D0777975

STOP INTERRUPTING ME!

A Practical Guide to Teaching Kids Their Manners

Rebekah McClure

STOP INTERRUPTING ME!
A Practical Guide to Teaching Kids Their Manners

ISBN: 9798523706189

Interior image design by: Stephanie Werner
Library of Congress Control Number: 2018675309
Printed in the United States of America

Praise for *Stop Interrupting Me:*

"Stop Interrupting Me was such a valuable read! Full of wisdom and practical insight on every single page. Buy it. Highlight it. Refer to it often. Your family will be blessed by what you glean and put into action."

-Candace R.

"Pointed, easy-read with valuable lessons for both new and veteran parents. Demonstrates scripture in the everyday "teachable moments" of parenting. Approaches parenting with humility, gentleness, and teaching or coaching. Thoughtfully written."

-Stacey B.

"It is WONDERFUL!! This book is a practical and thorough resource for all parents. It addresses a vast amount of real life situations, giving applicable advice and helps for training your child in all of them. I wish I had this book before my parenting journey started! I recommend it for all parents!!"

-Candice B.

"I love this book! It's so easy to understand and apply the concepts, especially since it's written from everyday hands-on experience. I know this book will be a blessing and a practical guide for all parents. I love how the lessons model the Christ-like character we are supposed to have."

-Christi M.

"This (pleasantly short!) handbook is full of creative ways to parent. I love the challenge to change our parenting methodology and equip our kids with "tools" for success. The examples provided for manners are creative... and fun! Highly recommend!"

-Eva T.

"This book has been an eye opener for me as a mother of 4. This valuable resource is a must-have for any parent. Many real life situations are discussed and there are doable suggestions. We have started implementing many of them in our family. I am happy to say that I have already started noticing positive changes in my children's behaviour. This book is a short read and is a step-by step guide to being more proactive in teaching our children. Highly recommend this book!!

-Christina P.

"This book was so helpful for me with my two littles. Sometimes I feel overwhelmed asking myself how to teach life skills and character traits like problem solving, patience, and helpfulness. This book perfectly answered that question for me and gave me a great springboard for the future. It's full of gems that are easy to incorporate into my family's day-to-day life. The short sections make it easy to read for busy parents. I'd highly recommend taking time to read through this little book and have fun practicing new skills with your children."

-Lexi M.

"Every parent needs to read this book! It's so easy to read yet full of valuable parenting tips. The topics covered are true-to-life with easy-to-apply solutions whether you have one child or ten. I love how the author incorporates Biblical principles into this guide. I'm going to start using this book to coach my own children on manners today!"

-Amie A.

"This book has been such an encouragement to me! With many practical applications, the wealth of information can be applied to any home. Inspiring, convicting, and relevant to our current day's struggle! The encouragement we all need to raise our children in love and peace!"

-Mary L.

To myself.
Because, trust me,
I'm the one who needs it the most.

To my husband,
This book is the way you
naturally parent our tribe of eight.
Thank you for guiding me back to
gentleness when I get off track.

Table of Contents

PREFACE: MY IRONIC DISCLOSURE AND HOW TO USE THIS BOOK

As a homeschool Mama to several little ones, I have a great deal of teaching to do. Besides the obvious subjects of reading, writing, and arithmetic, I'm also responsible for teaching my children skills for everyday life; like cooking, cleaning, organizing, and countless other tasks. Yes, children catch on to quite a bit all on their own, but taking the time to intentionally impress certain values upon their little hearts can shape the rest of their lives too. If I want to make sure my children learn something specific, I should be intentional in teaching it to them.

My 14-year-old son was my guinea pig. I can honestly say that everyone who knows him thinks he has a heart of gold. My 11-year-old, 9-year-old, and 6-year-old also blow me away with their tender hearts and incredible generosity. Starting at just 18 months old, I did some of the most basic ideas from this book with each of them.

Colossal Disclaimer Time! All of my children (and myself!) are still a work in progress! We have rotten attitudes and yucky behavior on a daily basis. I can ASSURE you that I need to read this book more than anyone. I still forget to slow down, listen, stay calm, and create a teachable moment.

While examples and stories make for great books, my intent was to keep this book short and to-the-point. Busy Moms need a quick way to get back on track with a fresh vision. It is my hope that this book will do just that.

Also, this book isn't exclusively about manners. It's also a how-to guide for developing quality character values in your children and teaching them important life skills. It will walk you through more than 50 exceptional manners and skills that will last a lifetime.

"Doing" is one of the best ways for children to learn. Through practice, pretend, and play, this book will show you how to solidify immensely valuable traits into your children's hearts and minds through actual hands-on practice.

My hope is that while you are using this book as a guide for teaching meaningful lessons, you'll connect with your child's heart. This is not a legalistic list of do's and don'ts. We can lean into our child's world for fun, play, laughter, and learning.

While the concept of "practice, pretend, and play" that is taught in this book is primarily for kids under age ten, you can certainly still implement these lessons with older kids as well. Older kids can always benefit from genuine, heartfelt discussions about these important topics. It's never too late to discuss valuable life skills with your kids through everyday conversations. If you are feeling like you have already failed your kids, you haven't! Skip ahead to chapter five to find the encouragement that is meant just for you.

Even though I'm going to give you numerous ideas for you to implement in your own home, you don't have to do all of them;

and perhaps you'll think of your own ideas to add to the list as well. After reading this book and mulling over the information, I encourage you to pick just a couple of ideas to start implementing in your home. These habits can't all be formed overnight. Take your time and don't let the sheer number of ideas overwhelm you. There is a learning curve for the parents here  too. It will take time to adjust your own habits and your own mindset. Parenting doesn't only involve children; a large chunk of the job is working on yourself.

INTRODUCTION: GIVE YOUR CHILD A TOOL

Do your kids ever exasperate the tar out of you? Do they ever drive you out of your ever-loving mind? You tenderly held your sweet little innocent buttercups when they were tiny babies. So how exactly, in the blink of an eye, did you get to this stage of constant sibling fights, selfishness, screaming, and bad attitudes that plum wear you out?

The typical knee-jerk responses to the annoying, unrighteous behaviors of our children are...

- "For the thousandth time, stop interrupting me!"
- "Stop fighting with your sister!"
- "Stop yelling!"
- "Don't touch that again!"
- "Don't hit your sister one more time, or else..."
- "Why do you have to act like this?"
- "What in the world is wrong with you?"
- "This is your last warning, stop it, NOW!"

I'm here to show you how you can teach your child (and yourself!) to have healthy responses to troublesome behavior. We really can gently and purposefully navigate the intense journey of raising a child who has a mind of his or her own!

At the end of the day, your relationships with your children matter more than the things you go to battle over... failure to do chores, messes left around the house, teasing of a sibling, not following orders, etc. So we should ask ourselves, "How can I navigate this situation and be able to successfully exit this conflict with all hearts intact?"

"How can I keep this relationship with my child in excellent condition?"

"How can I slow down in the heat of the moment, lower my voice instead of raise it, and keep myself calm?"

· **Slow down.** I must realize that there is no need to rush everything that I do. I need to lower my intensity level and give up on my demanding expectations.

· **Lower my voice.** Instead of raising it, I should take my voice to a whisper when the moments get tense. It's true that they'll "hear" a whisper far better than they will my yelling.

· **Keep myself calm.** If I can master any ONE thing from a library full of parenting books, I need to master this one. Calm. Down. Instead of acting as hysterical as my child who has lost control, I need to stay calm and remember that I am a mature adult. I have the power to bring peace to the situation. The rest of the day for my entire family may be decided upon by *my* ability to calmly handle the situation at-hand.

The other day I was nursing my infant while staring at my phone screen. I suddenly heard a fight break out right next to me. Isn't that how it always happens, suddenly?! Adalee, my two-year-old, had a toy that belonged to Hannah, one of my four-year-old twins. When Hannah saw that someone else was playing with her toy, she came over to quickly snatch it. Adalee held on tight, and in a matter of seconds, it was an all-out fight; a rotten, intense fight. Usually, when distracted with a screen, it's second-nature for parents to quickly lash out and yell, "Stop it!" But thankfully I was able to remind myself to stay calm. With 100% peacefulness in my voice, I said, "Hannah, why don't you tell her she can play with the toy for one more minute and then you'd like to have it returned to you?"

I handed Hannah a valuable tool: conflict-resolution. Within seconds, Hannah let go and repeated the phrase to her sister. Adalee then gently handed over the toy, stuck her thumb in her mouth, and sat next to Mama. The end.

How would this have gone differently if I would have just lashed out at them for being so loud and mean to each other? We both already know the answer from first-hand experience.

I'm well aware that your little ones may not have responded so well after some simple parental guidance. But because my girls have been practicing this from their very first days of playing with siblings, they can easily be steered towards kindness (usually!) Your kids can too. The secret ingredient is... YOU. It may take you several months of working at this, but you really do have the power to bring peace and harmony to your home. That may sound like the bad news, that the weight is on *your* shoulders, but it's actually very, very good news. Change can happen in the most stubborn child's heart if you're willing to make this one word your new life goal...

Teach.

CHAPTER ONE:
WAYS TO TEACH

When our children do wrong, we need to remind ourselves to *teach*. When our children are happy, content, and all is well in their world, we also need to remind ourselves to *teach*. Keeping this word at the front of our minds during every waking moment of parenting will yield incredible results. Instead of yelling, lecturing and using harsh words, we can calmly give our kids the skills they need to navigate any difficult situation.

Before we dive into teaching 50+ manners and skills, let's discuss some of the *ways* to teach these manners, character values, and life skills. How can we make sure our kids learn in a way that sticks with them for years to come?

Thankfully, there are several valuable ways to teach a child.

→1. **More is Caught Than Taught.** Your kids see the way you live. You could never say a word and your kids would still learn limitlessly from you- whether good or bad. Their little eyes see the way you respond to stress, handle conflict, and mend broken relationships. They see your humbleness... or pride. They see your gentleness... or harshness. They see how you spend your free time. They see how you treat others, especially your very own family. Observing you while you simply live your life certainly has the largest effect on their young hearts.

→2. **Character-Building Story Books.** Reading quality character-building books aloud to your children is another impactful way to teach useful lessons. It's important to discuss each story after reading it and apply it to real-life situations. Kids can learn amazing lessons from great books! Through reading out loud to your kids, they can grasp anything from honesty, to hard work, to loving their brother or sister. Next time your child is struggling with an issue, and after he is calm and open to hearing about it, remind him about an applicable story that you have read together. Discuss the problems and solutions from the book. What did the person in the story do that made for a great ending? (For a list of our family's favorite read-aloud books, see Appendix A).

→3. **Memorizing Scripture.** Practicing Bible memory is a sure way to impress important lessons upon your child's heart. By age five, my son had over 200 Bible verses memorized by heart. (See Appendix B to find out how). Your child can gain a wealth of wisdom and character through memorizing Scripture and discussing its meaning.

CADEN AGE 5 210 VERSES MEMORIZED

→4. **Bible Time.** The Bible is a treasure chest of golden nuggets waiting to be discovered. Reading Bible stories from quality Bible story books, as well as regularly reading from the actual Bible, will set up your kids to have a wealth of knowledge and compassion! Going through books of the Bible one by one throughout the years is a powerful way to teach your children. Reading Bible stories of courage and faith are inspiring for a child's heart. As an added bonus, reading the Bible aloud to your kids will have a profound impact on *you*. By breaking down verses and explaining them on a child's level, you will absorb an immeasurable amount of God's Word yourself. Family Bible Time may seem messy and you may think your kids aren't even listening, but having Bible Time in the home can produce miracle-like results. It may feel like such an intense struggle, but I challenge you to start with only 2-3 minutes, and watch all that God will do in their little hearts. (See "Staying

Quiet for Read Aloud Time" in Chapter Three for some tips on making it less hectic).

→5. **Teach In the Mundane.** I love the verse in Deuteronomy that talks about teaching your children when you lie down and when you rise up, when you sit, and when you walk by the way.[2] That pretty much tells us that *life* is a classroom; there's always something your child can be learning. Even while at play, valuable skills can be absorbed. We can also teach while we're driving, doing dishes, or putting a child to bed. Look for opportunities to apply and implement lessons from this book throughout your day.

→6. **Practice, Pretend, and Play.** Actually "practicing" manners, character values, and life skills allows our children to "do" rather than merely hear. Through practice, pretend, and play, we can be proactive parents instead of reactive ones! That, my friend, is a huge game-changer and the focus of this book.

Practicing situations outside of the moment is a powerful way for a child to learn.

Practicing situations outside of the moment is a powerful way for a child to learn. If we don't practice manners and skills when moments are calm, we are not setting ourselves up for success when the moments become tense. If you've practiced ahead of time with your kids, then the tense moments will be more easily navigable. Sometimes it will only take a gentle reminder of what your child has already learned to remedy a tough situation. Those moments are such a reward and a great return on your investment!

→7. **Conversations.** In addition, follow-up conversations about the practice that you've done, even when there are currently no struggles, is a great way to remind your child of the lessons learned. Bedtime or time in the car are great opportunities to have these conversations. Here a little, there a little. Especially for older kids, meaningful conversations will be the foundation for learning and improving character.

If you've practiced ahead of time with your kids, then the tense moments will be more navigable.

→8. **Do's Instead of Don'ts.** After an actual infraction or struggle, once hearts are calm and content, it's vital to discuss and/or practice how the situation should have been handled. More on this in Chapter Four. Instead of a long list of *don'ts,* we need to teach our kids what **to do** in order to correct a situation. Give them information that they can actually use for now and for the next time. Provide them with the tools and knowledge to do better. This is far more effective than cutting them down for what they have done wrong.

→9. **Praise and Encouragement.** Children also learn better if there is praise and encouragement present. As you work your way through the ideas in this book, make sure to do them with heaps of encouragement! Release and relax the scrunched-up, ever-so-serious-mom-face and remember to smile and offer praise. Make it a point to notice every single time your children show quality character. Compliment them for it. Lavish them with authentic praise! This will make all the difference in the world for your child's character development. More on this in Chapter Five.

While the focus of this book is to practice, pretend, and play, I must confess - I often shove "play" to the back burner so that I can get my "more important" tasks done. Proverbs 29:15 says that children left to themselves will bring their mother to shame.[2] Our kids need us to be there to work with them and even to play. We must engage. We must make it a point to invest in teaching stellar character. Nothing on our to-do list is more important than investing in our kids' lives.

We must remember to live in the moment we have in front of us right now.

A note about technology: We must be intentional about being present in the moment, and not constantly distracted. We must remember to live in the moment that we have in front of us right now. A short 12 years or so and their "little" years are over. Gone. The hearts of our children need more tending to than our phones and social media. Our children long for our presence and guidance; what beautiful opportunities we have right in front of us. There is nothing more worthy that you could do with your time and your energy than to give it to the people that you love the most.

Young children love acting and pretending. We can seize this opportunity by making it fun to learn manners and life skills. Your children want to play with you and you can do so while your children are learning amazing things.

Something else extraordinary happens when you take the time to teach children how to have quality character... you absorb the values also! Sometimes it's the parent who needs to learn patience, humbleness, and genuine kindness. At least, I know that is true for me!

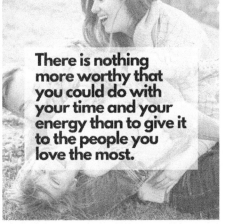

There is nothing more worthy that you could do with your time and your energy than to give it to the people you love the most.

Are you ready to "practice" with your children the manners that you want them to have, the character you want them to grow in, and the skills that will set them up for a lifetime of success? Let's dive right in!

CHAPTER TWO:
FUN MANNERS TO
PRACTICE WITH
YOUR CHILD

I've divided this book into three sections of ideas that you can do with your children: Manners, Character Values, and Life Skills. Several of them fit into more than one category, but no matter where they fall, pick one at a time to avoid being overwhelmed. Each one you do is an investment into your child's life. Let's begin with the ones that I consider "manners."

Practice Not Interrupting. You'll never again need to shout with utter exhaustion, "Stop interrupting me!" Your child can easily learn not to ask you a million questions while you're talking with another person. Here is how to practice...

Pretend you are conversing with a friend. If your child needs to tell you something while you're conversing, he should put his hand on your arm or leg and wait for you to answer. This is an amazing way for your child to let you know that he needs to tell you something. It avoids that incessant "Mama, Mama, Mama" while you're trying to have a conversation. That soft little hand can just rest on your arm or leg until you are ready. While conversing, you can place your hand over your child's hand to let him know that you are aware that he needs your attention. Explain ahead of time to your child what it means when you have placed your hand over his hand- that you will answer him as soon as you are able. If you practice this when you're not having a "real" conversation, it will be such a blessing to you and the person you are speaking with later. During practice time, praise him for waiting so patiently until you could take a break from your "conversation!"

Side story: My sweet little almost-3-year-old has put her hand on me several times before and I've made her wait and wait and wait. When I finally get a break in my conversation to ask her what she needs, she quietly says "pee pee." Know that sometimes you need to look down right away!

Practice Gentleness. Practice handing over toys kindly. Even if you have a tough football player in the home, you can nurture your child to learn the beautiful art of gentleness. Teach your child to say, "Here you go, brother" and hand over a toy very gently. Mama should go first to demonstrate. When a struggle comes along among siblings or friends, you can remind your child how to hand over toys gently.

Another aspect of gentleness is being careful with other people's possessions. Not only individual items around the house, but also being respectful of creations that others have made or built. If a child has built something out of blocks, set up a neat "campsite" in the living room, or made a cool art project, no one should come along and de-construct it or ruin it without gaining per-

You can nurture your child to learn the beautiful art of gentleness.

mission to do so. We can teach our children not to destroy things that others have made. It's a beautiful, touching sight to see a child use gentleness.

Practice Picking Up Dropped Items. Show your child how to quickly retrieve a dropped item and return it to its owner. Your child can do this for others at the store, around town, or in friends' homes. You can first practice at home. Let your child drop an item. Then you hurry to pick it up for him and say, "Here you go, son" as you hand it back to him. Next, you drop an item and let your child practice. After picking up the item, he can say, "Here you go Ma'am," and give it back to you. What a blessing!

Practice Answering the Front Door for Known Guests. Pretend to be a visitor to your own home. Go outside the front door and ring the doorbell. Have your child answer the door and greet you. Your child can offer to hang up your coat and invite you in to have a seat. What a delight!

Practice Taking a Knee. This is one of my favorite things to watch my kids do. We mostly do this when we are out playing with neighbors or at the park with friends, but also at home with siblings. When someone gets hurt, we all "take a knee" and let a parent tend to the hurt child. When the child rises up and feels a little better, all the other children can stand and clap for them before resuming play. This makes the injured child feel like a million bucks, sure to create a smile every time! It's very caring to pause the playtime when someone is hurt. We're learning to genuinely care about the feelings of others!

Practice Sitting Quietly. If you practice this, then the next time you need your children to sit quietly in a waiting room or at church, they'll know exactly what to do. Pretend you are having a church service or sitting in a waiting room. Have your children practice sitting politely. They should not wiggle down off the couch/chair or talk. Start with just 30-60 seconds. Next time, try two minutes. Over a few weeks, work up to 15 minutes or more. It is perfectly reasonable to let your children color quietly, look through books, or do something quiet with their hands during this time. You should sit close and also demonstrate sitting quietly. After the first session of 30-60 seconds, praise your children for staying so quiet!

Practice Introducing Yourself. Have your child practice introducing himself. Remember to be bold and friendly and to shake hands firmly. Say, "Hi, my name is _____. It's so very nice to meet you!" To go one step further, your child can think of a question to ask as a conversation starter. For example, "Are you enjoying the weather today?" "I like your shirt. Is blue your favorite color also?" Don't be surprised if you hear from others what a confident, friendly child you are raising!

Play the "My Pleasure" Game. When someone thanks you for something, it's extra sweet to say "It was my pleasure." To practice, you can thank your child for various things... "Thank you for cleaning the living room." "Thank you for helping your sister." To make this fun, you can even thank your child for silly things like, "Thank you for being so adorable and smiley." "Thank you for being as playful as a kitten." Your child can also thank you for various things so that you can lead by example in saying, "It was my pleasure." Both you and your child can have fun responding with this sweet phrase. Next time you have a "real" opportunity to use this phrase, seize the moment!

Practice Coming When Called. You can explain to your children that it is not efficient nor polite to yell from room to room. Instead, we should go near people to talk to them. Your child can practice coming near to talk so that it becomes the standard way of communicating in your home. Have your child go elsewhere in the house and explain to him that when you say his name, he is not to yell "What do you want?" from the other room. He is to quickly stop what he is doing and say, "Coming" while running/walking towards your voice. This will be such a blessing later. Parents should be the primary model of this by always remembering to go near the child to speak. If you are in the habit of yelling at your kids from another room, consider the long-term effects that getting up and going to them could have on the level of peace in your home.

Practice Receiving a Gift. Everyone loves receiving a "thank-you" and a compliment when they give gifts. Your child can develop the habit of having a grateful heart, while also making the giver feel appreciated. Get a used toy from around the house, put it in a gift bag, and present it to your child. Or siblings can pick out items for each other. You can even pick a not-so-fun item like a paperclip or a spatula! After opening the "gift," the child should practice saying, "Thank you" and one nice comment about it. Like, "Thank you for the paper clip, this will come in handy next time I have a stack of papers!" "Thank you for this lovely spatula. I can't wait to use it to flip pancakes!"

Practice Sincerely Apologizing. Oh if only the world knew how to apologize! Marriages would be healed and society would be more pleasant. There are four parts to a sincere apology. Anything less is not a full apology. Until these four parts become a routine habit in your home, you may want to make a chart with this information and hang it on your fridge. You can practice when there is no real conflict, so that it is easier when an actual struggle comes along.

→1. Start with a simple, "I am sorry."

→2. State what you did that was wrong. A quick, "I'm sorry" is not sufficient. We need to humble ourselves and admit the hurtful act that was done. "I'm sorry I hit your arm." "I'm sorry that I called you a mean name."

→3. Next, ask for forgiveness by saying, "Will you forgive me?"

→4. Finally, say, "What can I do to make it right?" Leave the offended person feeling satisfied that you did all that you could to remedy the situation. This shows that you are genuinely sorry. For example... replace or fix the item you broke, serve a snack to the person you hurt, or do a chore for the person you offended, etc.

Putting this all together: "I'm so sorry I took your favorite toy without asking. Will you forgive me?" "To make it up to you, is there something of mine you'd like to play with right now?"

If your child refuses to apologize in the actual moment of conflict, give them a few hours. Make a note to remind yourself to revisit the issue. Later, have a calm discussion, and ask again for a full, sincere apology. If a few hours wasn't enough, try again the next day. There have also been times where I have apologized on behalf of my child who did wrong. They couldn't bring themselves to admit their wrongdoing. So instead of punishing them or dragging this on for days, I will talk to all children involved. For example, in front of both parties, I will say, "Hannah, I'm so sorry your brother hit you. That was wrong and I know it really hurt. Is there anything he can do to make it up to you?" If he won't do the task, I am willing to help him do it or even do it for him. You may think this is being too "soft" on the offender, but I have found just the opposite. They are usually more likely to complete their own apology next time because they saw me humble myself on their behalf. As an added bonus, the offended person was acknowledged and heard, which is usually all they need in order to feel better.

Practice Sharing Your Things. I have twin four-year-olds. They model sharing (and fighting) over toys better than I've ever seen. We have practiced so much that even when a squabble does break out, I can usually talk through the sharing conversation with them (again!) and they will cooperate. We can explain to our kids how kind and unselfish it is to share. We can remind them that their siblings are their best friends and that our things are never more important than our friends. We should all learn to hold to our things loosely and to live a life with outstretched arms. You can practice this in your home by having your child go retrieve a favorite toy. Ask your child, "Have you asked your friend if she wants a turn with that toy? Do you think it would be kind to give her a turn? Then you could have it back." Encourage them to hand over the item gently. By "practicing" this skill, sharing will come more naturally when the "real" moment comes along. We all fight against selfishness, but you really can raise a mostly unselfish child.

Practice Giving Up Your Seat for Adults. Explain to your child that adults aren't usually comfortable sitting on a floor for long periods of time. It may make their back ache or their knee joints uncomfortable. So, when an adult comes into a room, children can learn to quietly move to the floor to free up seats for the adults. Practice this by entering the room when your child is in the comfiest chair. He should quietly get up to make the chair available. Next time you have an adult guest, they will feel flattered and honored that your child gave up their seat for them. There was no arguing, complaining, or even a conversation; he humbly and simply just moved to the floor.

Pretend Helping With Spills. If someone spills something, your child will be such a blessing if he knows to hop up right away and say, "Here, let me help you!" Your son or daughter hopping up to clean a mess can be a tremendous help to the family. When I've done well practicing and discussing this in my home, some of my little sweethearts will remember to jump up and help right away. I've especially made it a point to never make a big deal out of accidents like spilled food, broken dishes, etc. So, most of the time, when someone breaks a glass on the kitchen tile, several people in our home hop up to start helping and it's not a big event. We are still working on those that choose to stay in their seats! You can practice this by "spilling" something and letting your child jump up to get a rag and wipe up your "mess." This is a great way to practice for the real thing, because a home with children is most definitely a home with spills!

Practice Being a Gentleman. Even toddler boys can learn to pull out chairs for their sisters and mother. They can learn to open doors for the ladies in their life. Give him plenty of opportunity to practice this sweet act of serving so that this polite habit will form beautifully from a young age. Girls can also learn to help senior

31

citizens, their mom, or others carry in groceries, etc. When my little 3-year-old would do something like this, she'd proudly say, "I'm a gentleman." I'd smile at how cute she is and then remind her that she's a "gentle lady."

Practice Proper Mealtime Manners. It may seem silly, but I recommend practicing mealtime manners when there is no meal at the table! Teach your children to thank their parents for the meal, ask to be excused, put their own plate at the sink, etc. Here are 13 *Marvelous Mealtime Manners* that you can practice with your children. It might be helpful to create your own poster of these manners and hang it near the dining table. Each week, pick one manner to be your focus. After about 13 weeks, you might have some *very* polite eaters!

MARVELOUS MEALTIME MANNERS!

→1. Sit peacefully and respectfully. We shouldn't be tipping our chairs backwards or being silly with our arms.

→2. Let others go first when dishing up food, or take the initiative to serve others before yourself.

→3. Thank the chef for preparing your food.

→4. Do not grumble or complain about the food. Politely eat it as a compliment to the chef.

→5. Talk about pleasant things. Speak of things you're thankful for, great parts of your day, hobbies you've been enjoying lately, etc.[3]

→6. Talk in a calm, soft, peaceful voice. Avoid talking loudly. Do not be noisy or make loud noises with objects. Mealtime should be peaceful.

→7. Take turns speaking. Do not interrupt others.

→8. Say "Please" and "Thank You" when applicable throughout the meal.

→9. Take small bites. Do not overload your mouth. Avoid talking while food is in your mouth.

→10. Do not drink with food in your mouth.

→11. Be clean while you eat, try not to spill food or make messes. Slightly lean over your plate or bowl to take each bite.

→12. When you are finished eating, you can either stay and talk with your family or ask to be excused. Then take your dishes to the counter or sink.

→13. Offer to clean up. Ask, "What can I do to help?" Or, take initiative to clean up with no prompting from an adult.

.

CHAPTER THREE: QUALITY CHARACTER VALUES TO PRACTICE WITH YOUR CHILD

Now that we've covered some manners, let's discuss some character values that you can teach your kids. Again, some of these could also be considered "manners" or "life skills." Either way, they are great lessons to practice at home. And please remember, you can't incorporate all of these overnight. Choose one at a time and have fun with it.

Practice Going the Extra Mile. It's wonderful when your child learns to add abundance to everything he does, to have no bare minimums! Of course, most adults haven't even mastered this one, but it's still worth practicing. Ask your child to do something simple, and then ask him to get creative and think of one bonus action that he can do in addition to the original request. For example, "Caden, please pick up these toys." Caden would then proceed to pick up all of the toys, plus straighten the books on the bookshelf. Or he will pick up all the toys, and then sweep the floor as well. The opportunities are endless to go the extra mile! Parents can also model this daily to demonstrate its greatness.

Practice Responding Calmly To Frustrating Situations. One quotation I say often is, "It's okay to mess up; it's not okay to get angry about it."[4] Have your child pretend to mess up on something, perhaps handwriting or drawing, then have him show a proper response to his frustration. "Oh man, I messed up drawing this house. I guess I could flip the paper over and try again on the other side." He can practice not being able to lift something. Instead of getting angry or frustrated, have your child politely ask for help. "This is too heavy for me, can you help me, please?" Toddlers or preschoolers can simply say, "Help please." Practice the proper response to frustrating situations. You can gently remind your child of the proper response next time a frustrating moment occurs. Instead of anger being the default response, teach them to try to find a solution, or calmly ask for help.

As parents, we should also model this when we are frustrated. How beautiful it is for a child to repeatedly witness his parents responding calmly to frustrating moments! Priceless! You could lower the level of stress in your home tremendously by focusing on this skill yourself. Children learn oh-so-well by... example.

How beautiful it is for a child to repeatedly witness parents responding calmly to frustrating moments.

Maximizing Others. In life, when someone does something great, it's an exceptional habit to hand out encouragement and praise to them. Teach your child how to maximize others! Give your child various scenarios and have her think of a praise to say. For example, a cashier worked quickly while checking out your family. Your child could say, "You sure are a speedy cashier!" Children can practice this on their siblings... "You sure are fun to play with." "I like the way you made that creative village out of blocks!" We should look all around us and look for ways to maximize others.

Showing Humbleness. Pride is a sure way to lose friends. Some children are constantly bragging on themselves while cutting down others.[5] When we are on the receiving end of praise, we should learn to graciously accept the compliment and then deflect. We can use this as an opportunity to be humble. For practice, give your child a compliment. Tell your child something like, "You are such a hard worker! I can't believe you cleaned the whole living room!" He could say, "Thank you, it was my pleasure. You've taught me how to clean well." Or when the child is told they are so special and sweet, she can learn to say, "And you are so special and sweet to me too!" This simple skill will give your child a wonderful lifetime of friends! People love humble friends that aren't always using compliments to further boast of themselves.[6]

Just the other day, my little six-year-old spent the whole morning being so helpful and hardworking. He kept helping me with everything and it was a pure joy. When we got ready to leave the house, I asked him, "How did you get so helpful and sweet?!" He replied, "God made me that way and you 'teached' me how to help others." Oh my Mama heart! Our kids are listening, watching, and learning; they really are!

Following Instructions. There are five points to remember when teaching your child to follow instructions.

→1. Start right away when asked to do a job.

→2. Work cheerfully.

→3. Work without complaining.

→4. Complete the tasks thoroughly.

→5. Report back when the job is done.

As the parent, you should go first to demonstrate. Have your child give you a command. You should begin to execute the job and show her how to start right away. You should show cheerfulness while you work... by smiling, singing, humming, or just your attitude of pleasantness. Show your child what a thorough job looks like and that you didn't leave parts of the task unfinished. Point out to your child that you didn't make excuses, that you simply got the job done. Come back and tell her when your job is complete.

Then, give your child a simple command or two. You could say, "Haley, pick up the blue ball and the red block and put them in the toy bin." Walk her through the five parts of following instructions. Give her lots of praise and celebrate a job well done. When "real life" tasks come along, you can remind her how grand she already is at following instructions

Parental Anger. Give your child permission to calmly put his hand on your arm or leg if he ever feels like you are getting angry. When the parent is getting heated, a tender little hand is sure to calm things down. Give your child permission to say, "I think you're getting angry" or "I think you're having anger." A soft answer turns away wrath.[7] Mama can pretend to get angry and let the child practice notifying her, using his little hand. You should accept this gentle reminder as a clue to calm yourself down and be a good example of peacefulness in the home. Model the behavior that you want them to demonstrate. See Appendix C for 30 verses on anger that will have a profound effect on your home.

Also, it's beneficial to focus on not letting the behaviors of little people cause you to lose it. If their actions are causing you to be a mad woman, then you have less control than you think. Today, my 9-year-old was refusing to do her basic responsibilities. I could have become red-hot mad, but I recognized that she wasn't being outright defiant. She was lacking motivation, dreaming of playtime, and felt overwhelmed that she had so much on her list. Most of the time, your kids aren't being defiant for the sake of making your life difficult. Dig a little deeper and consider their feelings. I was able to navigate the situation with her by offering to help her. Without breaking her spirit, I held firm that she did need to complete her responsibilities. Using patience and kindness, we got the work done together. She felt loved, respected, and relieved that her chores were finally done. I didn't have to give one of those heartbreaking apologies for having harshness and being mean. Instead, she felt closer to me and more loved by me by the time we were done.

Taking Joy In Your Work. Practice doing chores and singing. You and your children can practice smiling while you work! You can "pretend" to wipe counters and pick up toys to make it funny. Make it a habit to sing and smile while working. Try setting a timer for 15-20 minutes and have the whole family make a conscious effort to work with joy. Until your family learns this art, focus more on the joy than the actual chores!

Play the "Initiative Game."[8] Teach your child to constantly be looking for ways that he can help. When someone is working on something, have him think about what the person might need next in order to do the job. Your child can get it ready. You might need a pan next while preparing dinner, and he can go ahead and get it out for you. Maybe you'll need an onion next

"**See a need, fill a need.**"

in your recipe, so he can go ahead and get it for you. Teach your children the meaning of the phrase, "See a need, fill a need." Spend some time looking for ways to make other's lives easier.

The No-Tripping Household. When a child leaves out a toy, it can hurt others who may later walk by and trip on it or stub a toe. Keeping our belongings off the floor is an act of kindness towards others. Have your child "practice" (several times a day!) putting away her toys so that others can avoid pain and injury. You can role-play this scenario by telling your child to put some toys on the floor. You can walk by and pretend to trip and get hurt on one of the toys. Feel free to act a bit dramatic. Explain that getting hurt is no fun, and that sometimes it takes days to recover from an injury caused by a toy that was simply left out on the floor.

Looking for Ways to Serve & Give. Have your children make a list of ways to serve others and be a blessing. Let them brainstorm ways they can give of themselves. Do some of the things on this list. Visit someone, bake cookies for someone, write a card, give away a toy, etc. You can "practice" doing these things at home or actually go do them! See Appendix D for a thorough list of great ideas!

Helping the Frustration. A quiet gesture of kindness is a great way to calm the spirit of a frustrated sibling. Have one sibling pretend to be stressed, frustrated, or struggling. The other sibling should quietly do something helpful or encouraging for her. A child can pretend to struggle to find her shoes. Another sibling can say, "Let me help you find them" and begin looking. The tendency is to get upset at the struggling sibling for being so loud and obnoxious. But sometimes, a simple, helpful task can immediately wash away their stress.

Practice Proper Tattling. If a child does wrong, his sibling should try twice to get the offender to listen and correct the wrongdoing. Parents don't usually need to be dragged into the conflict immediately. If the offender won't heed the advice, then the child can come and say, "Mama, I don't want to be a tattletale, but I encouraged him two times to do what is right and he won't listen…" That's tattling with the right heart! This can be practiced outside of tense moments. From now on, whenever a child comes tattling to you, you can remind him to go try twice to work it out with his sibling first.[9]

Pretend Caring for Someone Who is Hurt or Sick. Our kids can learn compassion and helpfulness through the practice of caring for others. One sibling or the parent can pretend to be hurt or sick while others think of ways they can help.

· "Do you need a glass of water?"

· "Can I get you a bandage or an ice pack?"

· "Would you like help getting up?"

· "Do you want a pillow to prop yourself up on the couch?"

When a sibling really does get hurt or is sick, remind the siblings of how to care for them.

Practice Serving the Poor or Homeless. We talk openly in our home about poverty, joblessness, alcohol, drug use, and even prostitution on a level that is safe for their little ears. We don't shy away from hard subjects. Kids will learn about these topics in one way or another. I'd rather my

MY TWINS AT AGE THREE. "SERVING THE POOR."

children learn about these from me. We've decided as a family to either give food to someone begging for help or to donate to a trusted organization that is already in place to help the homeless or impoverished. Organizations can sift through scams and truly help with food, housing, education, etc. I also want my kids to have a heart to go serve in these organizations. So we practice a sort of "soup kitchen" scenario at home! We like to set up a pretend grill by laying a box fan on its side using some books, blocks, or random objects to raise up the corners. We then tape little pieces of yellow, orange, and red party streamers to some of the slots on the fan. When the fan is powered on, the streamers will wave in the breeze, creating fun "flames" for grilling. We get out our pretend food, spatulas, and tongs. The kids love "grilling" for me while I hold my "hungry" belly and tell them how many days it's been since I've eaten. I get a little dramatic and tell them stories of "how hard life has been for me." They love to give and serve me all of their best food. They make sure I am as stuffed as possible. You could also do this with just a play kitchen. Watching my kids generously "give", even during play, melts my heart every time.

Doing Acts of Kindness for Each Family Member. Learning to serve our very own families is crucial to learning the second greatest commandment, to love our neighbor as ourselves.[10] Our siblings and our immediate family are our closest neighbors! Your children can help with a chore, serve a treat, or play a sibling's favorite game with them. There are endless ways that a child can do acts of kindness for his siblings. You can "pretend" or just actually do it!

Our siblings and our immediate family are our closest neighbors!

Acting Out Bible Stories. Acting out all kinds of Bible stories can solidify a certain character quality or lesson you're trying to teach. Using a simple Bible story book like "101 Favorite Stories from the Bible,"[11] we could easily choose one per week and have 101 weeks of stories to act out! Of course, you can keep it simple or you can dress up, use props, and set up a stage using furniture! The lessons your child will learn through acting out Bible stories will blow you away!

Staying Quiet for Read-Aloud Time. Children can learn to sit and quietly listen. Even if this takes an enormous amount of practice and dozens of gentle reminders to keep quiet, it is worth the work. Children should learn that talking, whispering, or noisily playing with toys is distracting to the reader and to the other listeners. It is okay to play quietly in the same room while listening to the book. You can practice this outside of the "real" moment by reading a book out loud that's not really on your list to get through for the day. It's very beneficial to practice outside of the actual moment when it will be needed the most. Start with a short snippet of just 1-2 minutes of reading and increase by 1-2 minutes each session. Praise them after each session, even if it was very short. Perhaps you could work your way up to 30 minutes in a couple of months or less.

Here are some activities your children can do with their hands while their ears are listening.

· Blocks that Snap Together
· Reusable LCD Writing Pad with Stylus
· Playing with Little Vehicles (Trucks, Cars, etc.)
· Stickers/Sticker Books
· Puzzles
· Setting up a Farm or Safari with Toy Animals
· Making Bead Necklaces (Chunky Beads for Younger Children)
· Playing with "Easter" Eggs (Snapping Trinkets Inside or Organizing by Color)
· Playdough
· Stacker Pegs
· Mail/Toy Mailbox Play
· Coloring/Drawing
· Lacing Cards
· Playing with Pretend Food
· Playing with Buttons/Color Sorting
· Sorting Dried Beans
· Making Greeting Cards from Blank Cardstock and Putting Them into Envelopes
· Writing on a Small Chalkboard with Chalk Markers
· Chalk Pastels on Construction Paper
· Doodle Art
· Spirograph Art
· Rubik's Twist Toy or Quiet Handheld Fidget Toy
· 5D Diamond Painting

Play the "What Can I Do to Help?" Game. Having a helpful heart is a priceless gift to others. If your child sees someone working on dinner or chores, it would be a delight if he would ask what he could do to help. Pretend to work on something and have your child ask if he can help. Encourage this wonderful habit by replying with very simple tasks that he can complete within 1-2 minutes. For example, your child sees you making dinner and asks if he can help. You ask him to get you out a large mixing bowl. He may ask again, and you can tell him you will need the measuring spoons. Let him help you and then praise him for doing so. You want him to ask again the next time, so make sure the tasks are do-able and not overwhelming. Over time, his endurance will mature so that he is able to help with longer tasks. If children are taught to look for opportunities to help, they will be a blessing indeed.

Play the "What Can I Do Next, Mama?" Game. Whether it be chores or helping a sibling, your child can learn to check back in with you after a task, before running off to play. For practice, give your child a simple command. When he has completed that command, he should ask, "What can I do next, Mama?" Then give him another simple command. Do this throughout your day. The commands can be a mix of serious and silly. Definitely include some silly! Later, when you have a "real" chore for him, remind him to come back and ask what else he can do next. What a servant's heart he is learning to have!

Self-Control. When treats are offered to children, we all know the typical reaction of most of them. They contend to be the very first child to receive said treat. Here is a great way to learn to wait and demonstrate self-control. Put a delicious treat in the middle of a table, or even on a plate on the floor, and have everyone sit around it. Ask your children to sit still with their hands peacefully in their lap; no reaching, grabbing, or begging for the snack. See who can sit there without grabbing or demanding the first turn. One by one the parent signals one child to take the tiniest little sip or bite and then set the remainder back down. The child should slowly and gently reach for the item and slowly and gently return the item to the center (unless it was already in tiny pieces and the piece was consumed). This is a time to show self-control by being calm and quiet. Continue this until the snack or drink is gone. Children can learn the lovely habit of self-control. Oh the rewards of not having ravenous grabbers every time treats are offered!

Responding to Getting Hurt. Another important time for a child to demonstrate self-control is when he is hurt. If you have a child that tends to scream loudly and overreact when he falls or sustains a minor injury, practice this skill. Pretend to get hurt and then hold your hurt spot while saying, "Help, this really hurts" in a medium-tone voice. Teach your child that it's okay to cry and say "help" at a reasonable volume level. It's not okay to scream like we need an ambulance when there is no gushing blood or broken bone. After several years of working on this with a particular child of mine, he no longer startles the neighbors when he scrapes his knee! Practice makes progress!

Having Patience With Others. Life isn't meant to be lived in constant hurry. Oh how we moms need to learn that we don't need to rush through everything. Your child (and/or you!) can practice being patient by pretending to wait on someone. Stand politely and just wait. Don't huff or puff or holler "hurry up." Practice politely waiting. The other person can be pretending to take a verrrry long time. Praise the patient child for waiting so long! Do this so often that it becomes a new way of living; a new lifestyle, an unhurried life.

Practice Honesty. Children should learn to come tell the truth right away. Give them situational examples and have them report the truth right away. For example, tell your child that he was playing with a ball in the kitchen, knocked over a glass from the countertop, and the glass shattered all over the floor. He should practice coming to you right away and saying, "Mama, I was playing with a ball in the kitchen. I knocked over a glass and it broke. I'm so sorry. What can I do to help clean it up?" Let him pretend to clean it up! Or "I hit my sister when she took my toy. I'm sorry.

I will ask for her forgiveness." A person who can be honest right from the beginning will save himself a lifetime of relationship problems.

Practice Winning. Bragging on ourselves is unpleasant for others to hear. Instead, when we win a game, we should glorify God for those strengths and think of compliments that we can say to the other players. Tell your child, "You just won at Connect Four!" Then ask her to respond like a true winner... "With God, all things are possible. You played such a great game, you almost had me on that last move!" The other player will know that she is safe to play with you again next time. Pride shouldn't take the fun out of playing. A humble winner is a true winner.

Practice Losing. Now practice how to behave if you lose. Shake hands and tell the winner, "Great game! I had fun playing with you!" It is a true joy to watch a child respond with such great character after losing a game.

Make Blessing Cards. It's so very sweet when your child can learn to make others feel loved and valued, especially a sibling. Help your child write a blessing card for one or all family members and set them nicely at the dinner table to be discovered by the recipients. This demonstrates kindness and thoughtfulness. It also builds family bonds, which is priceless! One of these blessing cards may become a keepsake and a remembrance of a special way that a child felt loved that day.

Practice Philippians 4:8. Teach your child that words are powerful. We can choose to say something lovely, or we can choose to say something destructive. Which option makes for great friends, a great day, and a great life?

Philippians 4:8 tells us to think on things that are true, lovely, virtuous, praiseworthy, etc. Practice saying something lovely and of good report even when it's hard to think of something. Even if your kids don't like certain things, they can still find something positive to say. For example, "Thank you for the broccoli, I was

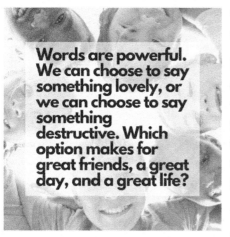

Words are powerful. We can choose to say something lovely, or we can choose to say something destructive. Which option makes for great friends, a great day, and a great life?

very hungry and this will fill me up."

Practice this by telling your child examples of situations that she would not typically be thankful for; like, "We can't go to the park today because it's raining." "All we have for dinner is rice." "Your favorite toy is broken."

The child should come up with something lovely to say even though she received disappointment. "I like rainy days. Can we play some card games?" "Rice fills our bellies, at least we won't be hungry!" "There are other toys I can play with, or maybe I can try and fix this one!"

Practicing this outside of truly disappointing moments can set the stage for real situations to end positively. We really can train our brains to think of positive statements rather than negative ones.

Practice Secret Giving. A good giver knows how to be anonymous. Practice some secret giving; like leaving a gift card on a car in a parking lot or leaving treats at neighbors' doors. You could bake something and play "Ding Dong Ditch." Leave the treat at a neighbor's door, ring the doorbell, then quickly run away so that you're not caught. There are all sorts of secret giving things you can do (See Appendix D). Be creative! And shhhh…the best kind of giving is done undercover! An even easier idea is to practice on family members at home. Like a professional sport, the amazing art of giving can only be mastered through practice.

Pretend to Visit a Hospital. Pretend visiting a sick person in a hospital. You can even have fun setting up a bed on the floor for the "patient." Wash hands before entering. Speak quietly. Take them a gift. Sit and talk with them if they'd like. Leave them with an encouraging word or prayer. You can practice all these caring acts at

home!

CHAPTER FOUR: LIFE SKILLS TO PRACTICE WITH YOUR CHILD

I am all about the practical. You can't get any more practical than actually practicing and preparing for difficult situations with your kids. Besides the ones in this book, you can also look for other areas of your family life that need help. You can actually put into practice the skills that are needed the most. Jot yourself little reminders of areas that need practice, conversation, or other methods of teaching. Find books or videos to help you teach certain skills. When you write down the areas that need attention, you are less likely to forget. When your kids handle a particular situation poorly, write it down and then practice it several times until it sticks. Here are some great places to start.

Practice Grocery Shopping. Many parents complain of exhausting trips to the grocery store. With some proactive parenting, you can minimize your stress. Practice at home! Get something you can use as a "cart" and push it around your house while you "shop." You can have your child practice keeping her hand on the side of your "cart." Then she can help you un-

With some proactive parenting, you can minimize your stress.

load and load your groceries. You can explain that you need to concentrate and then pretend to be muttering prices and ounces to yourself. Praise your child for being quiet while you were trying to save your family some money! Next time you go to the grocery store, you can say, "Remember how we practiced this at home? Let's keep our hand on the cart, let Mama concentrate, and I'd love your help when it's time to unload the cart."

If you have some children that typically ride in your grocery cart, you can also use this time to prepare for your next real shopping trip. You can assemble a special bag that includes an activity book, a fidget toy, etc. A few items that your child can use to keep her busy can be extremely helpful. Imagine the stress you can save yourself if you plan ahead.

Asking for a Compromise. We want to raise flexible, reasonable adults. Your child being able to ask for a compromise is perfectly reasonable. You can make him feel that his voice, opinions, and feelings matter; that you have no intention of railroading him or controlling him. Both the parent and the child can have their needs met in a healthy, respectful manner. By giving your child the power to ask for a compromise, you can save your home loads of strife. If the parent asks a child to do something that is out of line with what he thinks he should do, he can learn to ask for a compromise.

If you ask your child to do a difficult chore, he can say, "Instead of washing all of the dishes, may I do half of them, and then I'll keep the baby happy for a while?" Or your child may say, "May I politely tell you something?" This is respectful but also a way for the child to speak up about the situation if there is missing information or a genuine concern. He can politely give the information and ask for a compromise.

Be willing to let your child politely discuss with you the issues at-hand. Teach your child ahead of time what a compromise looks like, "May I finish this show before starting on my chores?" "May

I play outside for 10 more minutes before reading my book?" As a parent, try to be agreeable and reasonable as much as possible. Sometimes you just can't compromise, and that is okay. But most of the time, we can be flexible. Once both of you agree on a compromise, stick with it. Hold firm to the agreed-upon compromise. Compromises work wonderfully for ages 2 - 102!

Practice Praying With Scripture. It is a beautiful thing to hear a child pray using Scripture. It's a valuable art and act of worship! You and your children can practice taking Scripture and turning it into a prayer. An example of a verse that can be turned into a prayer is "Be ye kind one to another, tenderhearted, forgiving one another."[12] It can become "Lord, help me to be kind and have a tender heart. Help me to forgive others because you have forgiven me." Find some verses with your child and practice turning them into prayer or worship.

Practice Speaking In Front Of Others. Have your child practice praying out loud, reading out loud, or reciting things out loud for the family. This will help them gain confidence, public speaking skills, and leadership skills. A parent should go first to demonstrate. Start with very small snippets that are just one to two lines and work on increasing the length each week. Mama can recite something simple like, "Jesus is the Way, the Truth, and the Life."[13] The child can repeat this verse or think of her own. As the weeks go by, your child can practice reciting lines of her own choosing and work on lengthier recitations.

Re-Do's. We can obviously plan and prepare ahead by practicing as many character values as possible. But there are situations that will come up every single day that your child will handle poorly. In these cases, wait until their hearts are tender and no longer upset, and then GO PRACTICE THAT THING! If a child yelled from the other room when you called him, explain the better response and ask him to go back and try again. This solidifies the concept into their ever-learning brain.

In my home, we do re-do's several times a day; it's now a habit and second nature. Re-do's are a beautiful thing! Just a few minutes ago, one of my four-year-old twins walked up to my toddler, forcefully snatched away a toy, and said, "That's my twist toy." I explained to her how it physically hurts people's skin to have toys ripped from their hands. I explained how it also hurts people's feelings and makes them sad. I reminded her that her little sister is her special friend and that we need to treat our friends kindly. I asked her to apologize for not being gentle. She said, "I'm sorry I wasn't gentle, will you forgive me?" I asked her to re-do the toy situation again by saying, "I own that toy, may I have it please?" She reset the situation by giving back the toy. Then she asked for it politely. My toddler handed it over and we were done. Completely done! No long lectures, no shaming, no harsh punishments. The re-do IS the "discipline."

Did your child hit his sister when she called him a mean name? After everyone is calm and recovered, go back to the exact "scene of the crime" and practice what he should do next time that someone says something mean. Once he does this correctly, move on! No punishment is needed! Simply executing a re-do is a great way to solidify positive behavior. And don't forget to practice with the sister that said the mean words as well.

If your child refuses to do the re-do, try again the next day. You shouldn't just let it go, but you can certainly let him sleep on it before revisiting the issue. While sometimes it is good for parents to let some stuff go, it's also important to NOT let some stuff go. However, you can be willing to wait it out until all heads are cooled-off and all hearts are receptive. Keep a list on your phone of situations that need revisited. Write down conversations that need to take place. It shouldn't take more than a few days, but make sure that list is kept short and clear. You will get far better results if you simply record what needs work and then wait until everyone is calm before addressing it. Re-do's are a fantastic way to learn the proper response. After the re-do, everyone can move on with their day. Before or after the re-do, have a simple, heart-felt conversation about better response options for next time that situation occurs.

Give, Save, Spend. Wise money management is almost a lost art these days and it's so important to teach this skill to our children. Help your child set up three jars or pouches for learning how to manage money. This can be started at age three or so. Whenever they get paid commission for completing their daily responsibilities, doing extra jobs, or even receiving birthday money, help your children learn to divide it up into these three categories (suggested by Dave Ramsey): Give, Save, and Spend.

Help them use their "Give" money to give generously to needs around the world. Helping your children explore and recognize the world beyond themselves is indispensable. Talk about starvation, dirty water, malnutrition, lack of shelter and warm clothes, abuse, pre-born babies, etc. Let them contribute to these very dire needs. We have read *The Treasure Principle*[14] out loud as a family and it helped my children realize that "their" money is not their own. We are just managers for God, He owns the cattle on a thousand hills![15] He owns it all. We need to use it for His glory. Each "thing" that we own is only going to end up in a junk yard one day. But the treasures that we store up in Heaven will last for eternity!

Give your children a vision for the future.

Explain that their "Save" is for a future car, house, or college; as it's wise to avoid debt. Once your child has around $50 in his "Save" pouch, help him open a savings account or a mutual fund account. Four of my children have at least a couple hundred dollars in their own mutual fund accounts. They get so excited to make new deposits, purchase their own mutual funds, and check the balance every now and then. We've even used an online calculator to see what the balance will grow to be by the time they are 18 and even 60 years old. It's astronomical growth! Give your children a vision for the future.

Help them learn to use their "Spend" wisely, but allow them to make mistakes here and there. Mistakes are a great way to learn. One saying I often repeat to my children is, "If it's a good toy, at a good price, and you have enough cash; then buy it and enjoy it." If it's a cheaply made item that won't last, they probably shouldn't buy it. If the price is too high, they should keep an eye out for a better bargain. If the child has instantly decided he wants something the day he first sees it, encourage him to wait a few days to think it over. Encourage him to look at alternatives that might be more fun or that may save him some money. We can teach our children delayed gratification even while living in an instant-gratification world. I never loan my kids money, ever. It's good to have your children memorize the verse about having safety in the multitude of counsel.[16] Remind them when they're considering a purchase to ask a few people for advice. I also encourage my children to buy used items when possible, especially from garage sales, local For-Sale groups, and thrift stores. But again, leave the final decision up to them. It's better to make spending mistakes as a child and learn hard lessons at a young age than to make huge spending mistakes as an adult!

Chores. It's so beneficial for children to learn to help from a young age. A family unit is a team. A team must work together for the good of all members. But sometimes parents expect chores to be done well without actually taking the time to teach said chores. For at least the first 3-5 times that a child has a new chore (and maybe once every month or two after that!), the parent should do the chore WITH the child. Show them HOW you want it done. Don't despair if you have to "teach" the same chore 5-10 times even. Choose to stay gentle each time. Kindly teach the chore again like it's the first time the child is hearing this information. It's also very helpful to watch an online video of how to do the chore. My son watched a video on how to clean a toilet, and it totally clicked for him. He is now an expert toilet cleaner!

Parents can get so frustrated, annoyed, angry, and downright mean when their children don't do their chores, or don't do them well. But we hold the solution in our very hands. Walk through the chores with your kids. If you leave them to themselves to do a flawless job, you can perfectly predict that it's likely not going to happen.

What chore could you teach your child to do in order to make your home run smoother? Ideas include: folding laundry, cooking something simple for the family, taking out the trash, sweeping a floor, dusting, wiping mirrors or windows, tidying up the living room, etc. Pick just one chore this week to "teach." Take 20 minutes and break it down for them. I know this is investment parenting; it takes time and energy to teach. But the return on your investment is more than worth it.

Listening To Your Body. Sometimes it seems that a child can go a mile a minute without recognizing how he really feels... hungry, full, thirsty, tired, overstimulated, hurt, etc. You can teach your child to listen to his body for signals and clues so that he can do what is needed to be healthy and well-balanced. Explain to your child that sometimes we need to sit still for a moment, close our eyes, and really pay attention to how our body feels. Incorporating questions like these into your days can help a child learn to recognize what his body needs...

· "Is your belly feeling hungry?"

· "Stop for a moment and listen to your stomach. Has it had too much food this afternoon?"

· "Does your throat feel dry and need some water?"

· "Maybe your body would like some quiet time?"

· "If your body is feeling tired, how about we lay on the couch together and quietly read some books?"

· "Try to close your eyes and concentrate. Do you have pain anywhere? How do your legs feel? How do your arms feel? How does your head feel?"

· "Would you like to stretch and see how flexible your body is?"

· "You've watched a lot of TV today, do you think your body would like to get its heart pumping and do some exercise?"

· "We ate a lot of junk food this weekend, do you think our bodies would like some extra veggies today? What do your muscles and cells really want for lunch today?"

· "We've spent a lot of time indoors today, would your body like some fresh air and sunshine?"

Teaching your child to be able to recognize how their body really feels is the first step to their wholeness and wellness. Especially in our fast-paced society, people aren't paying attention to what their bodies really need. We eat, eat, eat and go, go, go. Show your child how to slow down, listen to his body, and meet the true needs of his body.

To give your child a desire to eat healthier foods, watch videos and documentaries together about nutrition. Read about the health benefits of veggies, fruits, beans, nuts, seeds, etc. My son saw a short 8-minute video online about how eating beans increases longevity of life. He now requests beans almost daily! Also, let your child help in the meal process by picking out produce at the store, looking up a recipe that sounds tasty to him, and preparing the nutritious meal himself. He'll be more likely to eat it if it's his own special choosing and his own hard work.

Exiting and Soothing a Melt-down. If you have any children at all, you know that meltdowns are a part of childhood, and even adulthood! That doesn't mean that we can't learn to handle them in healthy ways that encourage self-control, problem-solving, and finding calm. The best time to intervene in a melt-down is when it first begins. As soon as you notice the frustra-

Proactive parenting can save you all kinds of meltdowns!

tion mounting, jump in and offer yourself and your advice to help the child exit successfully. Before the next meltdown even occurs, be practicing techniques that your child can use the next time that he is losing control. Proactive parenting can save you all kinds of meltdowns! Here are some options both you and your child can use to succeed the next time he is losing his self-control. Discuss and practice as many of these as you can ahead of time.

→1. **Keep. Yourself. Calm.** If a meltdown has full-on escalated to absolute craziness or even terror, it is vital that you SHOW calm-ness to an overwhelmed child. If you are acting as out-of-control as they are, they will not learn how to calm themselves. Gather yourself and mumble this under your breath in those stressful moments, "I must remain calm. Breathe. I must be able to model this." Put on your own "oxygen mask" first.

I'll add here that sometimes we have to do a tough self-evaluation and ask ourselves, "Who is throwing the bigger fit here? Myself or my child?" Sometimes we react more out-of-control than the child having the meltdown.

Take some breaths, put in a pair of earplugs if you must, and gently lead your child out of the stress zone!

Children are going to do foolish things; they are still growing and maturing. As an adult, the burden of example-setting is on your shoulders. How will they learn self-control if it is not modeled for them? You've got this, Mama. Take some breaths, put in a pair of earplugs if you must, and gently lead your child out of the stress zone!

Yes, if the noise is ear-piercing, it may be beneficial to take the edge off by putting in a pair of cheap earplugs. When the noise level is lessened, you may be able to respond more calmly. Obviously, I do not recommend noise-cancelling headphones. Please make sure that you can still hear your child's voice.

→2. **At first, don't necessarily try to fix the problem at hand.** Your top priority is to work on getting them calmed. Once that is accomplished, you can help them with problem-solving.

→3. **Give calm guidance.** Sometimes you just need to calmly tell them what you *do* want them to do. My little 4-year-old Haley was fussing/crying tonight about not being able to reach her fruit. She was about to throw down her fork in frustration. I simply said, "Haley, let's be polite. You'll need that fork to eat. Why don't you stand up and move your plate closer so that you can easily reach it." She stood up and pulled her plate closer. She even smiled. Sometimes they only need some simple guidance.

→4. **Genuinely offer your child a snack or a drink.** This is not a reward. This is a way to help him calm down. Providing a snack or drink shows true grace and helpfulness, especially when you feel he is undeserving. Having that refreshment can really help a child's body to relax and regain composure. Even just a small glass of water can have an immediate calming effect. If a snack will get your child from point A (frustrated and overwhelmed) to point B (composed and calm), give him one. Don't withhold refreshments when your child needs to be refreshed!

→5. **Offer sensory activities.** Play-dough, sand play, water play, jumping on a trampoline, swinging, snapping blocks together, etc are all great sensory activities. This can be time together that can connect your child's heart to yours. It can put you in a position to teach to ears that are willing to listen. Even if you were demanding a task and they refused to comply, you can have a much sweeter time getting her to complete that task later by letting her chill-out with some sensory play first.

→6. **Try to turn the situation into a playful one.** Find something to laugh about, insert a tickle if you can. Children naturally love to play. Use this to your advantage. You can sneak playfulness into almost any situation, if you just try.

→7. **Move to a new environment.** Sometimes just going outside can lower the intensity of a situation. There's something about the sun, fresh air, and the big blue sky that can calm us fairly quickly. What a gift from God! This is why people go on nature hikes, vacation at beaches, and visit breathtaking scenery. It has a known calming effect. You could also hop in the car and go for a ride or just move to a different area of the house.

→8. **Nurture your child.** Hugs, massages, snuggles, just holding them on the couch; any of these things could give them the comfort and affection they need in order to feel loved, capable and secure. When my toddler is fussy and getting inconsolable, I often just place her on the counter next to me while I do dishes; she stays quiet and content for a good 30 minutes. Giving them that closeness can do wonders.

→9. **Praise and encouragement.** Find a reason to praise your child, even if it's something small that he did. At the first sign of a big breath, praise him for recognizing that his body needed some deep breaths. Or praise him for at least trying to fix the situation before he completely lost it. Praise him for something! When a child receives a genuine compliment from an adult, it is meaningful. It could potentially perk him right back up. There is much more on praise and encouragement in Chapter Five.

→10. **Show compassion.** Tell them you are sorry that they are struggling, that you are there for them, and that you will help them. Continue by telling them how much you care about them, and as a team, you will work on this problem together. They need to see you come alongside them to meet their needs. It's important to let them know that you are not mad at them, that you are on their side.

→11. **Don't rush into punishments, blaming, lecturing, yelling, or scolding.** This will only make things worse. Connect with their heart first. Then, from a state of calm, talk about how the problem can be resolved. Show grace as God does for you. No harsh punishments are needed. Most of the time, we can just re-do the situation and then move on and be done with it. No

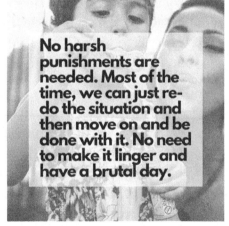

No harsh punishments are needed. Most of the time, we can just re-do the situation and then move on and be done with it. No need to make it linger and have a brutal day.

need to make it linger and have a brutal day. Lecturing, shaming, or yelling will only harden their hearts, and then no one wins.

CHAPTER FIVE: WORKING WITH A RESISTANT CHILD

There are several ways to be successful in teaching the valuable skills & manners from this book, even if your child is being resistant.

→1. **Be playful.** Make this fun. Don't force them to comply the way you want it done. It can be silly. There can be tickling involved.

If you try to use force and control as a parent, you probably won't be too successful. As children get older, they will exert their will. They will do what they want to do. If you are constantly trying to fight their will, you'll have tension in the home. But if you can work with your child on a conversational basis to bring all hearts to an agreement and to contentment, then you are modeling respect and will, in turn, gain respect. By not railroading your child's thoughts and opinions, you are showing that you value them and that you truly care about their feelings and their heart. We gain respect by giving it.

One hundred gentle reminders is more effective than one harsh scolding. It's more effective because you showed kindness, respect, and self-control one hundred times in a row ("seventy times seven").[17] Your children start to honor your requests because you have been respectful towards them, not using fear and force.

→2. **Model it.** Parents should model all of the manners first. Demonstrate to your child how to do each individual manner, skill, and character value.

→3. **Seize the real-life teaching moments!** When you see these skills or values demonstrated in "real life," point out what happened. Explain why they are so great and how they made others feel. For example, you witness a cashier being friendly with an angry customer, or you see a brother helping his sister down the slide at the park. Whenever you see honesty, hard work,  kindness, or another great quality demonstrated out in the world or on TV, have a conversation about it with your kids.

→4. **Schedule it.** Have a scheduled time carved out so that everyone is on the same page and knows what to expect. A sudden announcement of "Manners Practice" when they're not in the mood may not go over well. So for example, "Tomorrow after lunch, we're going to practice some skills from that book I've been reading." Or "Every day after lunch, we'll spend 5 minutes practicing proper etiquette. I'll make it fun for us!"

→5. **Lovingly, teach it anyway.** If they won't participate, you can do the acting or pretending using puppets or stuffed animals. Just *keep on keeping on* whether or not it seems like they are paying attention... they are! They can still learn these valuable lessons without actively participating. Ignore the crossed arms and the eye-rolls. They really are hearing what is happening. Puppets can especially add a new dimension to learning valuable content.

→6. **Offer a snack or drink to re-fuel them first**. Sometimes just some food or drink will change the mood or environment. We all enjoy feeling refreshed. While they are snacking, you can explain what the plans are for after snack time.

→7. **Give them transition time.** If they are doing something else, give them transition time. You can say, "In 10 minutes, I have a game I want us all to play. Be ready to go in 10 minutes." Then give a reminder at 5 minutes, 2 minutes, and 1 minute. By giving them this transition time, you are more likely to have willing participants. Demanding instant compliance when they were busy playing a game usually doesn't go over well. Keep the peace; give them transition time.

→8. **Lower your expectations.** Have grace, show grace. Change the ideas in this book to be more geared to your child's personality and age. Be flexible on when, where, and how to teach.

→9. **Engage differently with older kids.** If you have older kids who are too "cool" to participate, just let them be near the festivities and they will catch on. You don't need to force them to comply. Later that day, take some one-on-one time to maturely discuss the skill that you were teaching. Show them why it is important in real life. Explain how it's demonstrated in every-day situations. Always try to follow up with a conversation! Fill their week with gentle reminders of the skill discussed.

→10. **Above all, make these lessons peaceful.** Avoid battles over them. The Bible tells us to live peaceably with others and that "peacemakers" are blessed.[18] This starts at home. It is worth the effort to keep your home a peaceful one! Work with your child to gently teach and guide. Be willing to compromise and be flexible. Stay attentive to their needs and tweak these life lessons to tailor to them.

Hashtag Global. I often joke when I'm having a rough moment and I whisper to myself, "Hashtag Global." This means that I realize that my child's non-compliance is not something new. Children have been acting this way since the beginning of time. Maturity takes years to develop. If I can slow down and realize that parents all across the world struggle with these exact same attitudes and issues, I don't feel so offended when it happens to me. Remembering this helps me to calm down, step back, and come at it from another angle, or at another time.

I will even say out loud to my kids, but for my own benefit, "What you did is something that a lot of kids do. In fact, kids have been doing this for many years. It may not be wise but you're not the first person to ever do this. Many moms have had to experience this with their kids." Saying it out loud helps **me** to get some perspective. Coloring on the wall after being told not to do so, saying mean things when asked to do a chore, refusing to eat the dinner that was so lovingly prepared... there is nothing new under the sun![19] Maturity takes time. Doing foolish and immature acts does not mean that your kid is rotten. It means that he's... a kid!

Flying Objects! Recently, one of my kids was throwing some foam alphabet pieces across the living room and up to the ceiling. At first, I tried to ignore it since it wasn't technically causing damage or harm. However, somewhere along the line it really started to get on my nerves. I asked him to put the foam letters away. A few minutes later, he was throwing them again. He had been trying to see if he could get them all the way to the top of the soaring ceiling. I again told him to go put them away. Well, the throwing must have been too fun and exciting because he was soon back at it again. I could feel myself getting completely frustrated. I was DONE! It was driving me bonkers. I went over to him and placed my hand gently on his arm. I said, "I know kids like to have fun. I know kids like to throw things that fly through the air. I know that you are not damaging anything and that this is a fun game to play. But moms really like peaceful homes and this game is too hyper for me. You are welcome to throw balls outside but my head needs a break from flying objects in the house." Instead of accusing HIM of annoying me, I acknowledged that kids all around the word like to throw things, that it is normal and common. He didn't feel attacked and I didn't let an average kid's love of fun make me cast blame and shame upon him. It doesn't always end this well, but when I remember that one little hashtag, #Global, I can usually stay calm and realize that this is not some rare event. Next time you need to correct your child, feel free go ahead and say it out loud... "hashtag global."

Lastly, let's discuss praise. You must not forget that praise and encouragement are a hundred times more effective than badgering, lecturing, yelling, forcing, or demanding. The Bible repeatedly tells us to build each other up, including our very own kids.[20] Remember that your job is to coach. You are not a drill sergeant or a dictator. You are your child's biggest cheerleader and positive challenger. A good coach is an encourager. I've even hung a handwritten chalkboard sign on my wall that simply said, "Coach." What a magnificent one-word reminder.

Do you want to know what happens when I tell my little Hannah that she is so helpful? She tries to find ways to be even more helpful. If she does a small task and I acknowledge her helpfulness, she asks, "What else can I do to help?"

Even earlier today, my 6-year-old decided to do his sister's chores with zero prompting from me. I complimented him on his hard work and initiative. I told him that he has a "heart of gold" and explained to him what that phrase means. A few minutes later, as he shut off the vacuum cleaner, he said, "When you tell me that I have a heart of gold, it makes me want to do more nice stuff."

Praise generates great character.

Also, in front of the other children in the family, I will compliment a child. The other day I said, "Hey family, do you know what Hannah asks me every day? She says, 'What can I do to help, Mama?'" Because I acknowledged this publicly, she does it even more. And so do the other children! All because of a brief moment of praise.

If you call your children "honest" when they demonstrate honesty, and "hardworking" when they work hard, you might just raise some honest, hard workers! Look for the good and speak life into your children.

Back when I only had one daughter, I would call her "Sweet Girl." Even when she was in trouble, I'd say, "Sweet Girl, we cannot do that." I still call her the same name even though I have five daughters now. And do you know what? She's a very sweet girl! Coincidence? Probably not. Calling your children meaningful nicknames is such a treasure.

Whenever I have taken my children somewhere fun and we are departing, my Emily always remembers to say, "Thanks for taking us." It melts my heart every time. I always reply, "Aww, I love that you always remember to say 'Thank you.' You have such a thankful heart!" It's our routine and I'd say one feeds off the other to make a beautiful cycle of thankfulness.

Here are some more great examples of praise and encouragement...

· "Yay Haley, you did such a thorough job cleaning up that spill."

· "Great job, Luke, you showed compassion to your brother when he was hurt! That was so very sweet of you!"

· "You are so polite. I love practicing manners with you!"

· "That was great initiative buddy, I didn't even ask you to clean up that mess!"

· "I love seeing you be so cheerful and full of joy. Your smile is the best!"

· "You encouraged your brother when he was discouraged, that is so awesome!"

· "Thank you for being so sincere when you had to apologize. That showed a truly tender heart."

· "I love how honest you are! Thank you for telling me the truth!"

· "You avoided an argument with your sister. You are an amazing peacemaker! I appreciate that about you!"

· "You have got to be one of the hardest working people I know. Wow, you really cranked out that job. Thank you!"

· "I noticed that you didn't fuss or complain when I told you to start your chores. That means so much to me."

· "I saw how gentle you were with your sister. I love it when you are gentle!"

· "Aww, melt my heart. You let your brother go first. Thank you for being so kind."

· "You are so creative, you came up with that all by yourself, wow!"

· "Way to keep your things organized so that they are easier to find when you need them. That keeps your items in great condition too."

· "You have some major endurance, you've been working diligently on that for a really long time!"

· "I saw you show courage. That wasn't an easy thing to do but you were brave and did it anyway. Great job, buddy!"

CHAPTER SIX: HOW WOULD JESUS PARENT?

As much as I've loved writing out all these parenting tips and techniques for teaching our kids, I would be totally missing the mark if I didn't share with you the best parenting advice on the planet. We often don't recognize Bible verses as "parenting" advice; we assume that they apply to how we treat others outside of our home. Without much thought, we assume that verses about being kind and "loving our neighbor" only apply to how we treat the rest of the world. When in reality, the most important people in our life should be receiving the best fruit of our walk with Christ! When you intentionally look for it, you can apply so much Biblical advice to how you treat your very own children. This has been eye opening for me! Here is some parenting advice directly from the Word that I have hand-picked to focus on in my parenting journey. I challenge you also to slowly look at each of these verses individually through the lens of parenting.

- Love your neighbor as yourself. Matthew 22:39
    - Our children are our closest neighbors!

- Try to live peaceably with all men. Romans 12:18
    - And all children.

- Blessed are the peacemakers. Matthew 5:9
    - Not the hysterical, screaming, angry parents.

· Have compassion on others. Love them like your brothers. 1 Peter 3:8
  · Especially your very own children.

· In all that you do, do it in the name of Jesus. Colossians 3:17
  · Every diaper change and every meal prepared.

· Genuinely have a tender heart. Ephesians 4:32
  · Even when your life with little people is difficult.

· Do good to all men. Galatians 6:10
  · And children.

· Don't complain and argue. Philippians 2:14
  · Even to/with your children.

· Provoke your children to love and to good works. Hebrews 10:24
  · Not to anger or shame.

· Don't discourage your children. Colossians 3:21

· Be considerate of others. Hebrews 10:24
  · Especially those that are smaller than you.

· Be completely kind. Ephesians 4:32
  · Don't be mean to your kids by yelling, using sarcasm, or being rude. Kindness matters.

· Edify & encourage others, let your words be a gift. Ephesians 4:29, Romans 14:19
  · Build up your kids!

· Speak pleasantly, with grace in your voice. Colossians 4:6

· Use pleasant words that are sweet to your child's soul. Proverbs 16:24-25

· Have joy! Philippians 4:4; Proverbs 17:22; Psalms 118:24

· Smile often! Don't keep that joy down in your heart, show it.

· Be willing to be patient. Galatians 5:22
　　· Even during intensely frustrating moments.

· Be humble. James 4:6, 10
　　· Even if you are the one in charge.

· Be gentle. Galatians 5:22; James 3:17; Ephesians 4:2
　　· Both with your actions and your words.

· Avoid long lectures. Proverbs 10:19

· Have self-control, anger is foolish. Ephesians 4:29, 31a; Ecclesiastes 7:9
　　· (See Appendix C for 30 verses on anger).

Let's look at one more useful passage of Scripture.

Most of us know the fruit of the Spirit in the following two verses, but they really grip me in regard to how I treat my very own children. I have taken the time to slowly chew on this and I invite you to do the same...

"But the fruit of the Spirit is:

· Love
　　· Am I being loving? Or does my voice come across as harsh and cruel?

· Joy
　　· Am I grumpy? Or am I smiling and singing and being playful?

· Peace
　　· Am I yelling, bickering, and lecturing? Or does my demeanor bring a calming peace to the home?

- Long-Suffering
  - Am I truly being patient? Or do I expect my family to jump at my every whim and command? Do I expect them to rush around as quickly as I do?

- Gentleness
  - Am I rough and rash with my words and my body language? Or am I sweet and tender even in the tense moments?

- Goodness
  - Am I causing harm and hurt feelings? Or am I working for the good of others in my home on a daily basis?

- Faith
  - Am I living like I trust in the Living God? Or am I so wrapped up in my own worries that I don't show dependability on Him daily through His Word and prayer and worship? Do my kids see me walking out my faith?

- Meekness
  - Am I humble? Or do I march around like the commander of an army? Am I often insistent that I'm right or am I willing to apologize even to my toddlers and teens when I didn't handle a situation well?

- Temperance
  - Am I able to control my anger and not lash out at those I love the most? Or do I treat them badly just because I can? Am I modeling the self-control that I expect them to have?

Against such there is no law." Galatians 5:22-23

The very first place that we should be living out the Gospel, loving others, serving others, giving to others, and having the fruit of the Spirit, is in our very own home.

It is possible to parent your kids with compassion, as brothers and sisters in Christ. It's a beautiful thing to treat them with tenderness and politeness. Kids are important people. You'll never regret treating them the way you would like to be treated.

CONCLUSION: SHOW THEM WHAT YOU DO WANT

There are no guarantees with parenting. Your child will grow into an independent person that makes her own choices in life. She may choose a different path than what you'd like. She may "go astray" and break your heart by her adult choices. But if your child can look back and say, "My parents made me feel so loved and respected," then you have done a tremendous job.

Helping a child mature and develop with quality character values intact is one of the most difficult tasks on the planet. We need to slow down, recognize and remove distractions, work on our own issues, and treat our children the way we want to be treated. People may shout that children are inferior and need to be obedient to their parents. I would argue that children will willingly obey and comply if they are treated as well as the parents are treated, or as well as the parents expect to be treated.

What about removing those "distractions?" Your toddler screaming for a toy is not a "distraction." Your teenager huffing and puffing is not a "distraction." Your eight-year-old wanting you to color with her, your son wanting you to play "town" with him, your baby needing to be held... these are not the "distractions" of your day. These are the main things! All the other random to-do items are the "distractions." Remove, delegate, or streamline them. Pay attention to the hearts of your children first. This is a valuable investment into something that actually matters years down the road, unlike your day-in and day-out duties.

If you are working through baggage from your past, grief and heartache from a loss, depression, anxiety, or another tough issue, it is so important that you make it a priority to keep connecting with the hearts of your kids. You may be walking your own valley, but this is the only childhood they get. Help them learn to live fully, love big, and cherish all the blissful things about life. Stop and tell them precise things that you're thankful for. Ask them what they are thankful for. Make gratitude flourish in your home. A thankful heart is a gift your child can use to get through any dark valley in life.

I hope this little book was helpful to you. Remember that teaching your children what you DO want them to do, rather than harping on them when they do wrong, is most effective and beneficial. "Teaching" is proactive parenting at its finest. And by simply taking time to "practice," you can give your kids the gift of stellar character.

Demonstrate.
Practice.
Re-do.
Discuss.
Model in everyday situations.

· Demonstrate what you want to see.

· Practice it together.

· Re-do a situation when there's a problem.

· Discuss it with heartfelt conversations.

· Model these valuable skills yourself in everyday situations.

These intentional parenting techniques will surely solidify great principles in your child's life! The level of peace in your home will greatly increase if you can adopt these core concepts!

APPENDIX A: OUR FAVORITE READ-ALOUD BOOKS

I've read approximately 200 chapter books out loud to my kids. Listed below are my very favorite ones! Quality character-growing stories like these are amazingly powerful for teaching meaningful life lessons. I would rather invest my money into life-impacting books than plastic toys, electronic gadgets, and more clutter. The precious discussions I've had with my kids because of these books makes them worth every penny.

Uncle Arthur's Bedtime Stories- Volume One thru Volume Five, by Arthur Maxwell. Each of these five books contain small short stories that can be read in five minutes or so. Each story teaches a valuable character lesson. These books are old so they hold so much more innocence than many modern children's books. My children have learned so much from Uncle Arthur!

The Bible Story- Volumes One thru Ten, by Arthur Maxwell. Written by the same author as the books mentioned above, these books also contain short stories that are quick to read aloud. They are amazing at bringing the Bible "alive." The stories are captivating for children and adults alike. They are sure to inspire your child's heart and mind.

Books by Bob Schultz. These books are so valuable for boys that are age five and up. Each chapter is just 2-4 pages and teaches a valuable character lesson like hard work, honesty, going the extra mile, having wisdom, etc. My boys (and my oldest girl!) have loved these and learned so many neat concepts from them. Bob Schultz is a common name around here, we often talk about the stories from his books. The three titles are: *Created for Work, Boyhood & Beyond,* and *Practical Happiness.*

Heaven for Kids, by Randy Alcorn. This book will give your kids such a real, tangible feel for what Heaven will really be like. And it's so exciting! My kids now talk about what they'll do in Heaven; the games they'll play, the places they'll travel, the people they'll meet, the foods they'll enjoy, the hobbies they'll have, the landscape features they'll explore, and the animals they'll play with. This book is a family favorite!

The Treasure Principle, by Randy Alcorn. When I complete a great adult book on my own that I think will teach my children valuable lessons, I read it to them too. We did only 2-3 pages at a time of this book because it's so rich! We had the best family discussions about possessions, money, generosity, storing up treasures in Heaven, etc. My kids now have such a heart to live with open hands and to honor God with their time, talent, and treasures!

Christian Heroes Then and Now, by Geoff and Janet Benge. These are for ages seven to ninety-nine. My kids are on the edge of their seats as I read these out loud to them. Almost every single one we've read (over 30 of them so far) have blown me away! These are powerful stories of adventure and sacrifice. Mostly missionary biographies, these stories will open the eyes of your children to a world far beyond themselves. Our favorite ones are: George Mueller, Eric Liddell, Jacob Deshazer, Corrie ten Boom, Gladys Aylward, Nate Saint, Lilian Trasher, Charles Mully, and Sundar Singh.

Apologia Young Explorer Series. Although these are science books, they are so engaging to read aloud as a family! My kids have developed a love for God's amazing Creation through these books. They now have such neat interests in animals, plants, and astronomy. Our favorite titles are: *Exploring Creation with Astronomy, Exploring Creation with Botany, Swimming Creatures of the Fifth Day, Flying Creatures of the Fifth Day,* and *Land Animals of the Sixth Day.*

101 Favorite Stories from the Bible. This book is shorter than the

Bible Story book series mentioned earlier. Each Bible story is just one page long with three comprehension questions after each story. Each story has a great illustration and delivers the story true to the actual Bible. We have used this book as a springboard to act out Bible stories ourselves.

.

APPENDIX B: HOW TO TEACH BIBLE MEMORIZATION

Shortly after turning 5 years old, my son Caden had 210 Bible verses memorized by heart. I remember the first Bible verse I ever gave my first child, to see if he could say it... "Seek, and ye shall find." (Matthew 7:7). It was right when he was learning to talk in phrases, right around age two. Little fella impressed me by easily memorizing it and walking around saying it. My second son was the same story. By age 6 ½, he had 354 Bible verses memorized! I don't think I ever realized the potential for young children to learn so much and memorize so much! Wow! And truth be told, it's been a piece of cake to help them memorize all these verses! Children absorb so much if you just practice with them.

How have they done it? How can you teach your children to memorize Bible verses?

→1. **Start when they are young!** Two-year-olds can start to learn very simple, short verses.

→2. **Start with simple verses.** Choose ones that are short and easy to pronounce. See below for some ideas.

→3. **Introduce the verse.** Tell them that it's a brand new one, to really listen well. In segments of only 2-3 words at a time, have them repeat it after you. Once they are comfortable with that, have them repeat 4-5 words at a time. Then see if you can start the verse and they finish the whole thing. Continue to say this verse over and over for the next 7-14 days or until they know it well.

→4. **Add one at a time.** Add just one new verse and practice it 1-10 times a day for several days, until it is mastered. Then pick a new one!

→5. **Exclude the reference information.** I don't make my children memorize the location where it is found in the Bible (e.g., Galatians 5:1). That's just not as important to me as knowing the actual Scripture words themselves.

→6. **Review.** Each week, review all of the verses that your child already knows. This will mean that there are never any "old" verses. All of them stay fresh in their memory from the time they learn them until the time they leave home! Keep reviewing ones they know. Never stop!

→7. **Make them visible.** When they were little, all of my children's memory verses were on index cards taped to our wall. I knew that if I put them away, we wouldn't say them nearly as often. If you do this, you might find your child standing at the wall one day by himself reading them without being asked. It will melt your heart! As we added more verses (and more kids!), we did have to finally transfer the older kids to laminated pages with about 20 verses per standard page. They currently read two pages of their memory verses each day Monday through Friday. This is written on their daily homeschool list so that it is not forgotten.

→8. **Practice the verses anytime, anywhere.** Whether in the car, at the store, bedtime, during play time, or at the park, recite some verses.

→9. **Make songs out of them.** A large number of my children's memory verses have some kind of rhythm to them that we created ourselves. Singing makes them more fun and easier to remember! The verses sung to a tune are our favorite ones.

→10. **Keep it fun.** I let my children jump on the trampoline while saying their verses. Or I give them a jar of marbles and for each verse they say, they get to take one marble out of my jar and fill up their empty jar. Or they get to jump off the couch each time they say a verse. Create games so that practicing is fun!

→11. **Keep challenging your child to learn more and more!** Be encouraging and watch their memory capacity expand! What a precious gift to give your child! Before they leave your care for an adult life of their own, they can have 100 – 1,000 verses of Scripture hidden in their heart! Wow! If you do nothing else as a parent, this alone is an amazing gift to give!

→12. **Discuss the meaning.** Lastly, don't forget to discuss the verses and what they actually mean. Give real life examples and break down the verses so that they are well understood. When you experience something in life that could tie in with a verse that they know, talk about it! Show them the application.

An added bonus is that YOU will learn all of these incredible verses and they'll be hidden in YOUR heart too! Truth be told, that's been my most favorite part of teaching my children Bible verses!

Beginner Bible Verses

· If sinners entice thee, consent thou not. Proverbs 1:10

· Let all your things be done with charity. 1 Corinthians 16:14

· He that hath the son, hath life. 1 John 5:12

· Seek ye the Lord while he may be found, call ye upon him while he is near. Isaiah 55:6

· Hear instruction, and be wise. Proverbs 8:33

· Honor thy father and thy mother. Deuteronomy 5:16a

· For I will declare mine iniquity; I will be sorry for my sin. Psalm 38:18

· The joy of the Lord is my strength. Nehemiah 8:10b

· Seek and ye shall find. Matthew 7:7

· Every good gift and every perfect gift is from above. James 1:17a

· A wise man will hear and learn. Proverbs 1:5a

· A wholesome tongue is a tree of life. Proverbs 15:4a

· Thy word is a lamp unto my feet, and a light unto my path. Psalm 119:105

· And God said, let there be light: and there was light. Genesis 1:3

· Be ye kind one to another tenderhearted, forgiving one another. Ephesians 4:32

· But with God all things are possible. Matthew 19:26b

· I am not ashamed of the gospel of Christ. Romans 1:16

· Trust in the Lord with all thine heart. Proverbs 3:5a

· It is more blessed to give than to receive. Acts 20:35b

· For whatsoever a man soweth, that shall he also reap. Galatians 6:7

· But the fruit of the spirit is love, joy, peace, longsuffering (patience), gentleness, goodness, faith, meekness, temperance (self-control). Galatians 5:22-23

· Fear God, and keep his commandments: for this is the whole duty of man. Ecclesiastes 12:13b

· Be glad in the Lord, and rejoice,... and shout for joy. Psalm 32:11a

· And having food and raiment let us be therewith content. 1 Timothy 6:8

· O taste and see that the Lord is good. Psalm 34:8a

· Be of good courage, and he shall strengthen your heart. Psalm 31:24a

· The fear of the Lord is the beginning of knowledge. Proverbs 1:7

· Depart from evil, and do good. Psalm 37:27a

· Create in me a clean heart, O God. Psalm 51:10a

· All things work together for good to them that love God. Romans 8:28

· For the Earth is the Lord's and the fullness thereof. 1 Corinthians 10:26

· In the beginning God created the heaven and the Earth. Genesis 1:1

· The fear of the Lord is the beginning of wisdom. Proverbs 9:10a

· All our righteousnesses are as filthy rags. Isaiah 64:6

For more verses that are great for Bible memorization, visit my list at... https://bekamcclure.wordpress.com/2021/04/30/more-bible-memory-verses/

APPENDIX C: 30 VERSES TO HELP PARENTS WITH ANGER

Yelling and flipping out is "common," but that doesn't make it healthy and right. A hundred gentle reminders is better than one harsh scolding... Not that it should take a hundred reminders, but Jesus did say to forgive seventy times seven. A harsh scolding is never a great way to handle a young heart.

You can break the chains of anger!

It's a tremendous help to memorize these verses one by one and hang them around your home and car. However, even after intensely chewing on these verses, I regrettably do still get angry at my kids when I'm not being mindful of what I know about anger and God's Word. Our home still gets stressful because of my expectations and demands. By my rushing around and being critical, I cause hurt feelings. It breaks my heart! While we should do some intense work on our own heart, and we should memorize these verses and post them as reminders, we will still mess up. When we fail, it's so important that we sincerely apologize. Asking for forgiveness mends precious relationships in a beautiful way. Being willing to apologize to your kids is huge. Not only does it teach them humbleness and how to apologize when they do wrong, but it brings justice and healing to their hearts too. They feel validated and valued. If you're not willing to apologize to your kids when you do wrong, they will likely grow up and have some bitterness toward you or they'll simply keep their distance from you. A sincere apology is immensely important.

Here are some amazing verses to help you conquer anger...

· "He that refraineth his lips is wise. In the multitude of words there wanteth not (lacks not) sin." Proverbs 10:19
　· More words means sin is more likely to occur. Less words = less verbal sin.

· "A fool uttereth all his mind: but a wise man keepeth it in till afterward." Proverbs 29:11
　· Keep it in till afterward. Don't speak out of anger! Wait for the emotions to settle.

· "An angry man stirreth up strife, and a furious man aboundeth in transgression." Proverbs 29:22
　· Parental anger causes more problems than the child's original infraction.

· "Seest thou a man that is hasty in his words? There is more hope of a fool than of him." Proverbs 29:20
　· Don't jump to conclusions. Stay calm and evaluate the situation. Sometimes we aren't seeing the entire situation clearly, it may be different than what you know to be true.

· "Let every man be swift to hear, slow to speak, slow to wrath." James 1:19
　· Slow to speak! Take a break or at least some big breaths before speaking.

· "He that handleth a matter wisely shall find good." Proverbs 16:20
　· Go for the gold, Mama. What a prize and honor to handle parenting situations wisely.

· "He that keepeth his mouth keepeth his life: but he that openeth wide his lips shall have destruction." Proverbs 13:3
　· Avoid destruction, be the watchman of your own lips.

· "It is an honor for a man to cease from strife: but every fool will be meddling." Proverbs 20:3

> · What can you do to stop an argument? Do that!

· "Suffer not (allow not) thy mouth to cause thy flesh to sin." Ecclesiastes 5:6a

> · Don't let your mouth cause you to sin!

· "He that is slow to wrath is of great understanding: but he that is hasty of spirit exalteth folly" Proverbs 14:29

> · It's foolish to lash out in anger.

· "A soft answer turneth away wrath: but grievous (harsh) words stir up anger." Proverbs 15:1

> · Talk softly to your family, even in the stressful moments!

· "Be not hasty in thy spirit to be angry: for anger resteth in the bosom of fools." Ecclesiastes 7:9

> · Anger towards your family is foolish.

· "Pleasant words are as a honeycomb, sweet to the soul, and health to the bones." Proverbs 16:24

> · Talk pleasantly to those in your home!

· "He that is slow to anger is better than the mighty; and he that ruleth his spirit (is better) than he that taketh a city." Proverbs 16:32

> · Be in control of your own self. Rule your own spirit and you'll be mightier than he that conquers a city.

· "Keep thy tongue from evil." Psalm 34:13

> · Don't use your tongue to speak cruel, destructive words that pierce your child's heart.

· "Let all bitterness and (all) wrath, and anger, and clamor, and evil speaking, be put away from you." Ephesians 4:31

> · Get rid of the wrath and anger in your voice and in your body language.

· "Not that which goeth into the mouth defileth a man; but that which cometh out of the mouth, this defileth a man." Matthew 15:11

> · Our angry words are what defile us!

· "He that is cruel troubleth his own flesh." Proverbs 11:17

> · When we degrade those in our very own home, we end up hurting ourselves.

· "Be not rash with thy mouth, and let not thine heart be hasty to utter any thing before God: for God is in heaven, and thou upon earth: therefore let thy words be few." Ecclesiastes 5:2

> · Avoid the endless lecturing. Let your words be few.

· "But now ye also put off all these; anger, wrath, malice, blasphemy, filthy communication out of your mouth." Colossians 3:8

> · Get rid of all these destructive habits! This includes swearing or vulgar words.

· "Let no corrupt communication proceed out of your mouth, but that which is good to the use of edifying, that it may minister grace unto the hearers." Ephesians 4:29

> · Spread grace, not harsh words! These are polar opposites! Edify your kids.

· "The ornament of a meek (gentle) and quiet spirit, which is in the sight of God of great price (precious)." 1 Peter 3:4

> · A gentle spirit is of great price to God. Be a gentle person.

· "A fool's voice is known by multitude of words." Ecclesiastes 5:3

> · Sometimes even Mama needs to zip it!

· "The discretion of a man deferreth his anger; and it is his glory to pass over a transgression." Proverbs 19:11

> · Defer your anger! It's to your honor to overlook a transgression someone has done to you. You don't have to go to battle over every little thing... overlook it!

· "He that is soon angry (quick-tempered) dealeth foolishly" Proverbs 4:17a

> · Don't suddenly lash out in anger, try patience first.

· "Whatsoever things are true... honest... just... pure... lovely... of good report; if there be any virtue (anything virtuous), if there be any praise (anything praiseworthy), THINK ON THESE THINGS." Ephesians 4:8

> · Look for the good in your kids. Don't focus on all their wrongs. Avoid being critical. Build them up by noticing all that is lovely about them.

· "Be ye kind one to another, tenderhearted, forgiving one another." Ephesians 4:32

> · Be especially KIND to those in your own home! Kindness doesn't only apply to friends outside of our homes.

· "Whose keepeth his mouth and his tongue keepeth his soul from troubles." Proverbs 21:23

> · Keep your mouth under a watchful eye. You'll save heartaches if you can hold in the critical words that you were thinking about speaking.

· "He that hath no rule over his own spirit is like a city that is broken down, and without walls." Proverbs 25:28

> · Have control over your own behaviors and actions. If you are a loose cannon, you will have brokenness in the home.

APPENDIX D:
A (Nearly) Exhaustive List of Fun Things To Do With Your Kids!

Never be bored again. Sift through dozens of ideas from our family to yours. Here are ways to serve others, activities to do at home, places to go, games to play, outdoor activities, fun educational activities, and more! We keep this list handy and refer to it often for ideas. Life is so very short, soak up all the moments you can with your kids while you still can.

> **"Enjoy the little things in life**
> **because one day you`ll look back**
> **and realize they were the big things."**
> **-Kurt Vonnegut Jr.**

Ways Kids Can Serve
· Serve your family at meal time.
· Serve dessert to your guests.
· Pick a chore and do it with a willing heart.
· Do something nice for each family member (make their bed, serve them a snack, give a foot massage, etc).
· Pray for someone who is sick or in the hospital.
· Read a book to a younger sibling.
· Practice letting others choose first.
· Write a card welcoming a new neighbor.
· Give bottled water to construction workers.
· Pray whenever you see or hear an ambulance.
· Buy an item for a cashier and let the child hand it to her after bagging.

- Help pick up trash at stores, buildings, parks, or anywhere you go.
- Deliver cinnamon rolls to someone.
- Color a picture for a missionary and send it.
- Visit a sick person in the hospital.
- Visit a nursing home. Take large print Bible verse cards to hand out to residents. Prepare to sing loudly.
- Visit a homebound person, take them a colored picture.
- Deliver a dessert to a neighbor.
- Mail a card of encouragement to someone.
- Write a special note to someone.
- Pass out Gospel Tracts at stores or around town.

Fun Places to Go- Mostly Free

- Visit every park in your area.
- Go to work with a parent.
- Have fun with ropes at a local park. Bring ropes and learn knot tying. Raise or lower "treasures" to the top of the playset from the bottom. Climb or swing with ropes that you have properly tied.
- After a rain, play in a creek.
- Visit every state park within two hours of your home.
- Go to a sand volleyball court or a nearby lake with a beach and play in the sand.
- Go camping. You can either just camp for a "day," or stay 1-2 nights. Build a fire and make memories.
- Go geocaching, take small items to trade.
- Plant a new geocache in your area and give it a fun name.
- Go explore for bugs or flowers.
- Go throw rocks in a lake.
- Go swimming. (Health Tip: Avoid chlorine and cancer-causing chemicals. Look for natural swimming areas or salt water pools without hydrochloric acid).
- Fly a kite using a giant kite.
- Play tennis on a local tennis court.
- Go on a nature hike.

· Take a notebook and watercolor paints to a nature spot and paint something that you see.
· Find a park with pea gravel. Bring buckets and shovels and have hours of gravel fun.
· Play with stones. Find neat rocks, pick out special ones. Arrange them, display them, paint them.
· Play soccer or kickball at a nearby field.
· Find a zip line at a local park.
· Play at a local splash pad. Bring buckets, spouts, sprayers, and tubes.
· Take a 100-300 piece puzzle to a restaurant and have a parent/ child date night.
· Play baseball, have batting practice, or just play catch.
· Have a "watermelon picnic" at a park. Bring a watermelon and a large knife. Have fun eating the juicy slices while sitting on a picnic blanket.

Things to Do At Home- Indoor

· Make an indoor play town/village. Let someone be the restaurant owner, librarian, sherriff, etc.
· Give piggyback rides.
· Have fun doing foot launches. Lie on your back and raise your child up into the air with your feet. Gently launch them off your feet onto a pile of pillows/blankets.
· Play music and square dance with each other.
· Wrap your favorite stuffed animal in a special blanket and care for it.
· Play dress-up and take pictures (fireman, police, army, chef, etc).
· Make homemade play-dough and play with it.
· Bake cookies or another treat together.
· Tell jokes and laugh together; look up some new jokes!
· Do exercises like headstands, lifting light weights, mountain climbing, crunches, etc. Make an exercise dice game by getting two larger foam dice from a dollar store. Glue a fitted piece of cardstock to each side of each dice. With one dice, write a different exercise on each

side. Write the numbers 5, 10, 12, 15, 20, and 25 on the different sides of the other dice. Take turns rolling both dice to see what exercise everyone will do together and how many repetitions.

- Play indoor camping. Use stuffed animals, blanket hideouts, indoor tents, etc.
- Play with a kids play-parachute.
- Play flashlight hide-and-seek after dark.
- Learn to juggle.
- Watch a show on a big projector screen.
- Play with trains and make a train village.
- Play "mail." Write notes to each other and have a "mailman" deliver them to your various homemade mailboxes around the house. Be sure to reply to the letters you receive!
- Look through old memory boxes of stuff.
- Look through old pictures or family albums.
- Sing hymns together.
- Make up a skit and act it out.
- Pray together.
- Swing your child in a blanket. With an adult holding each end of the blanket, the child swings inside like a hammock.
- Read children's books while snuggling on the couch.
- Have a Lapsit Time. Hold your child while you sing songs and read simple books together. You could sing songs like, "Jesus Loves Me," "If You're Happy And You Know It," "I've Got the Joy Joy Joy Joy Down In My Heart," "Oh Be Careful Little Hands What You Do," "I Love You Lord," "He's Got the Whole World In His Hands," etc.
- Give your child a pillow sandwich. Lay a pillow on the floor. Let your child lay on his belly on the pillow. Place another pillow on top. Apply a comfortable amount of pressure to the top pillow.
- Hold your child and sing while you bounce on an exercise ball.
- Give each other foot massages.

· Give each other foot baths. Wash each other's feet.
· Have water pouring fun at the kitchen table. Make sure this is structured and supervised or your kitchen will be a wet mess!
· Gather up some little toys like animal figurines or vehicles. Randomly split them up amongst the participants. Set up a trading game where you trade for your favorite toy cars or animals.
· Fix each other's hair, even allowing your children to fix your hair!
· Make homemade bubbles and blow bubbles.
· Make treasure hunts with homemade clues to find various items around the house.
· Play *Simon Says*, "Mama Says," or "(Child's Name) Says."
· Make paper airplanes that fly far. Look up how to do it with a rubber band!
· Practice hand-lettering/doodling with calligraphy markers.
· Make homemade business cards as if each child owned their own business.
· Paint with tempera paint on a canvas. Use a drawing book and draw your picture with pencil on the canvas first. Outline it with black marker before painting. When you are done with the main painting, outline your hand-drawn item(s) using a tiny paint brush and black paint. Hang each creation when you're done!
· Follow some online painting lessons.
· Play with chalk markers on small, individual chalkboards.
· Make all kinds of swirls and designs using a spiral maker set.
· Play with stamps and ink pads.
· Use random/leftover craft supplies to make a unique piece of art.
· Use fancy scrapbook paper and make elegant cards for others.
· Using permanent markers, color a neat picture on a clear, transparent page. Crinkle up a ball of foil, then straighten it back out. Tape the foil behind your transparent drawing for a stained glass window effect.
· Cover a piece of cardstock paper with small, colorful pieces of

tissue paper, using glue. Draw or trace your handprint, an animal, or other object onto a piece of black construction paper. Cut out your drawing and glue it on top of the tissue paper page. You now have a piece of art that looks like a stained glass window!
- Play with stickers.
- Draw new pictures with how-to-draw books… animals, vehicles, fruit, etc.
- Do some color-by-number pages.
- Do some color-by-sticker mosaics!
- Draw with chalk pastels after looking up some neat ideas online. Have fun smearing your colors for a soft effect.
- Make and play a homemade bowling game.
- Make homemade pottery using a kids pottery wheel.
- Make bead necklaces.
- Watch some videos that were made using hundreds of thousands of dominoes. They are magnificent works of art. Then play with dominoes!
- Play with lacing cards or another stitching activity.
- Learn to sew by hand or use a sewing machine. Make a homemade pillowcase or simple bag.
- Learn to crochet and make some simple crocheted necklaces. Watch some videos to learn how to make a pot holder.
- Assemble your own music band with structured music (and headphones!)
- Learn to play a simple song using handbells.
- Sort and play with colored buttons.
- Set up a marble race game.
- Make sand art.
- Play with kinetic sand and enjoy the rich sensory input! Use sand molds and make a village.
- Send your child a card in the mail. Or get a pen pal and correspond with each other.
- Play with a big pot of cold spaghetti noodles.
- Have your child lay on a blanket on a hardwood floor. Drag the blanket around while your little one enjoys the free

blanket ride.
- Build a big fort.
- Parent "wheelbarrow." Have your child lay down on their belly. Hold their ankles while they "walk" around on their hands.
- Have a game night with snacks and your favorite family games.
- Have a movie night with popcorn.
- Make homemade slushies. Use one cup of frozen cherries, 1 tray of ice cubes, 2 Tbsp fresh lemon juice, 1-2 Tbsp agave nectar, and enough water to blend smooth. Blend until smooth! The most delightful treat!
- Play charades.
- Throw a small, squishy ball back and forth in the house. Kids love to toss with their parents!
- Tell stories of your childhood.
- Leave hidden notes for each other.
- Make silly faces and take pictures.
- Pretend to be various employees, animals, etc. Make flashcards that say things like mailman, fireman, astronaut, giraffe, cow, etc. Everyone does the pretending for a few minutes and then someone chooses another flashcard for everyone to try together.
- Serve pretend food to each other. One person pretends to be poor while the others host a free store where the poor can come to get food. Your child could also pretend to "grill" some food and serve it.
- Play healthy doctor/chiropractor. Prescribe healthy food, vitamins, rest, water, and exercise!
- Play camping (homemade tents, teddy bears, toy camping supplies, etc).
- Pretend campfire cooking. Roast some yummy "food" over your "fire pit."
- Play fireman/policeman.
- Play "Boats." Your child gets in a container and scoots across the "ocean" (kitchen floor) with all their supplies loaded in their ship with them.
- Play soldiers/army/marching.

- Use coins/debit cards for pretend shopping at your home grocery store. Use a check-out lane, cashier, and a bagger who will bag the groceries. Make sure you use something that beeps for your checkout lane. Make sure you tell the customer to have a great day!
- Play baby/nursery. Use stuffed animals or baby dolls and care for them.
- Play with puppets.
- Play simple card games like *Go Fish, War*, etc.
- Play board games that you already own or consider learning/buying one listed below...
- Memory Match Game
- *Tic Tac Toe*
- *Stick Man (Hangman)*
- *Dots and Boxes*
- *Sudoku*
- *Hand Stack*
- *Egyptian Rat Slap* (Uses one standard deck of cards, look up instructions online!)
- *Connect Four*
- *Sorry*
- *Bingo*
- *Yahtzee*
- *Checkers/Chess*
- *Uno*
- *Scrabble*
- *Skip Bo*
- *Battleship*
- *Twister*
- *Monopoly Deal*
- *Cover Your Assets* (a family favorite at our house!)
- *Play Nine*
- *Ticket to Ride*
- *Blokus*
- *Rummikub*

Things to Do At Home- Outdoor

· Have an outdoor carnival. Each participant creates their own carnival game using supplies from around the house; bucket toss, target shooting, bowling, etc. Pay tickets to play each other's games. Be sure to have someone run a concession stand with drinks and snacks. Popcorn costs one ticket!

· Play a game of baseball, catch, or an exciting game of *Pickle*. Kids love to run from base to base trying to avoid getting tagged by a parent in the game of *Pickle*. Several kids can all play at the same time with two adults as the base players.

· Play soccer or kick ball.

· Toss and catch tennis balls.

· Water Play- either a water table, a small pool, a sprinkler, a slip-n-slide, or pouring in containers.

· Add sand to your water play. A sand/water table can keep kids busy for a long while.

· Play *Tug-Of-War* with rope.

· Play a family basketball game or a shooting game of *Pig* or *Horse*.

· Parachute play.

· Painting out in the driveway- either on large posters or paper from a roll, with washable paint.

· Watermelon picnic in the front yard. Sit out on a picnic blanket and eat watermelon slices.

· Have an overnight backyard campout.

· Have an evening backyard campout, not overnight.

· Climb trees.

· Create an outdoor treasure hunt.

· Go rollerblading/skating.

· Go on a family bike ride.

· Play field day games- sack race, 3-legged race, balloon toss, hula-hooping, etc.

· Projector night outside. Take a projector outside and play a movie.

· Have some rope fun- tie knots to make swings, to lower down

buckets, etc.
- Jump Rope. *Double Dutch.*
- Build something in the garage or work on an old motor. Take apart something old and explore its parts.
- Draw with sidewalk chalk. Make an outdoor obstacle course with circles to hop on, paths to navigate, etc. Draw roadways, stop signs, and even city buildings.
- Make a car from a cardboard box.
- Jump on a trampoline, parent and child together.
- Cut out wooden letters or animals with a scroll saw.
- Have egg hunts with empty plastic eggs, anytime of the year.
- Have fun with orange traffic/sports cones. Make obstacle courses, trick challenges, etc.

Fun Learning Activities

- Look through a picture dictionary together.
- Have read-aloud time.
- Do a science experiment.
- Quiet individual reading times for the whole family for 30 minutes.
- Have a spelling bee.
- Write a letter to someone.
- Learn something fun on the piano by watching online piano tutorials.
- Get some counting toys. Set them up and trade or play with them. You can make families, villages, or even play "Congress" by acting out various roles within the government.
- Play a fun math game. Popsicle sticks are great for learning tally marks. Make your own multiplication/division bingo. Count out beads. Make piles of 5 or 10 and do some skip counting.
- Make your own letters bingo, sight words bingo, or phonics bingo.
- Make a fun grammar game. 1. Match up contractions ("don't" and "does not," for example), synonyms ("huge" and

"large"), and antonyms ("hot" and "cold"). 2. Write one word on several index cards and then help your child put the cards in alphabetical order. 3. Write various nouns, adjectives, adverbs, prepositions, etc on index cards and help your child sort them into their proper category; a pile for

nouns, a pile for adjectives, etc.

· Quiz each other in geography (while learning a few new countries or capitals).

· Do some Youtube learning (places to visit, music composers, landforms, how things are made, etc).

· Do a puzzle (from easy 25 piece ones to harder 300-500 piece puzzles).

· Draw mathematical hexagons, septagons, octagons, etc! Draw a circle with a compass. Draw a radius on your circle. Divide 360 by the number of sides you wish to make (a fun octagon is 360/ 8, so 45 degrees for each angle). Use your first radius to measure your first angle (45 degrees in this example). Use that radius to draw your next angle, etc. Connect all your end points and you will have an octagon! Color it, cut it out, and glue it on a popsicle stick for some fun play.

· Word searches.

· Mazes on paper.

· Dot-to-dots.

· Research something that you're curious about.

· Family Bible trivia.

**If you've enjoyed this book,
it would mean a great deal to me
if you would leave a review.
Blessings to you and your family!**

ABOUT THE AUTHOR

Hi, I'm Beka! I'm a homeschool mom to eight amazing kids. Four of them are little girls, ages 4 and under! I fiercely love Jesus and my family. My home is always busy and there is rarely a dull moment. I know that life is short and am determined to make each day count. I try to give my finite time and energy to things that actually matter. Besides Jesus and my family, my other passions include: nutrition and healthy living, a little bit of weightlifting, reading books, loving on grieving widows, fighting for medical freedom, exploring pivotal theology, sleeping, and writing in my journals. I keep a Thankfulness Journal and a "Write the Word" Journal where I write out God's wonderful blessings as well as Scripture that blows me away, encourages me, or challenges me. I also enjoy daily superfood smoothies and superfood salads, the necessary staple foods that keep me going!

To be notified when my next book releases, subscribe at the link below. It will be packed full of gentle parenting hacks that will make your days peaceful, connected, and blessed! I also have a book coming that will be for ages 8-15 that will be about health, true nutrition, and how to care for a growing/developing body! https://bekamcclure.wordpress.com/

You can also find me on Facebook at https://www.facebook.com/BekaMcClure

Works Cited

[1] Deuteronomy 6:7, KJV- "And thou shalt teach them diligently unto thy children, and shalt talk of them when thou sittest in thine house, and when thou walkest by the way, and when thou liest down, and when thou risest up."

[2] Proverbs 29:15b, KJV- "...but a child left to himself bringeth his mother to shame."

[3] Philippians 4:8, KJV- "Finally, brethren, whatsoever things are true, whatsoever things are honest, whatsoever things are just, whatsoever things are pure, whatsoever things are lovely, whatsoever things are of good report; if there be any virtue, and if there be any praise, think on these things."

[4] Hansen, Brant. 2020. Being Unoffendable: The Ridiculous Idea. Retrieved From https://www.faithgateway.com/being-unoffendable-the-ridiculous-idea/

[5] Maxwell, Arthur S. (2006) *Uncle Arthur's Bedtime Stories*, Volume 5.

[6] Proverbs 27:2, KJV- "Let another man praise thee, and not thine own mouth; a stranger, and not thine own lips."

[7] Proverbs 15:1, KJV- "A soft answer turneth away wrath: but grievous words stir up anger."

[8] Proverbs 15:1, KJV- "A soft answer turneth away wrath: but grievous words stir up anger."

[9] Proverbs 26:20 & 22, KJV- "Where no wood is, there the fire goeth out: so where there is no talebearer, the strife ceaseth. The words of a talebearer are as wounds, and they go down into the innermost parts of the belly."

[10] Matthew 22:39, KJV- "And the second is like unto it, Thou shalt love thy neighbour as thyself."

[11] Miller, Ura. (2007). *101 Favorite Stories from the Bible*. TGS International.

[12] Ephesians 4:32, KJV- "And be ye kind one to another, tenderhearted, forgiving one another, even as God for Christ's sake hath forgiven you."

[13] John 14:6, KJV- "Jesus saith unto him, I am the way, the truth, and the life: no man cometh unto the Father, but by me."

[14] Alcorn, Randy. (2001). *The Treasure Principle: Unlocking the Secret of Joyful Giving*. Multnomah Books.

[15] Proverbs 50:10, KJV- "For every beast of the forest is mine, and the cattle upon a thousand hills."

[16] Proverbs 11:14, KJV- "Where no counsel is, the people fall: but in the multitude of counsellors there is safety."

[17] Matthew 18:22, KJV- "Jesus saith unto him, I say not unto thee, Until seven times: but, Until seventy times seven.

[18] Romans 12:18, KJV- "If it be possible, as much as lieth in you, live peaceably with all men." Matthew 5:9, KJV- "Blessed are the peacemakers: for they shall be called the children of God."

[19] Ecclesiastes 1:9, KJV- "...and there is no new thing under the sun."

[20] Hebrews 10:24-25, KJV- "And let us consider one another to provoke unto love and to good works." 1 Thessalonians 5:11, KJV- "Wherefore comfort yourselves together, and edify one another." Ephesians 4:29, KJV- "Let no corrupt commu-

nication proceed out of your mouth, but that which is good to the use of edifying, that it may minister grace unto the hearers." Romans 14:19, KJV- "Let us therefore follow after the things which make for peace, and things wherewith one may edify another."

NOTES:

NOTES:

NOTES:

NOTES:

Made in the USA
Coppell, TX
19 October 2021

64318550R00069